This book offers a useful survey of Durkheim's theory of suicide from the perspective of present day sociology. It is an introductory work that disentangles layers of interpretative threads around this key text, and provides a notable framework for understanding the relevance of Durkheim's foundational text for today.

Stephen Turner, *Distinguished University Professor, University of South Florida*

This is one of the most interesting books on Durkheim in recent years, let alone one focused on Durkheim's foundational text. The book outlines Durkheim's categorization of "types of suicide" very clearly, and the underlying theory of socio-cultural integration of societies. It not only helps sort through the layers of interpretation around Durkheim's text that have built over the years in a helpful way, but introduces its own, and new, critique of Durkheim's analysis; and moreover, it offers some ways to clarify Durkheim's meanings on some of the ambiguous statements that he made in *Suicide*. It offers something new for today's readers and students, and shows how this pivotal, founding sociology text is still relevant to today's society and our understanding of it.

Jonathan H. Turner, *University Professor of Sociology, University of California, Santa Barbara*

REVISITING DURKHEIM'S SOCIOLOGY OF SUICIDE

This book explicates Durkheim's theory of suicide, reveals its ambiguities and contradictions, and sets forward a new framework to unify its various hypotheses.

Since Durkheim never fully integrated his theory, this has led to varying interpretations of Durkheim's theories among scholars, and subsequently, this caused a failure to create a cumulative body of findings about suicide due to inconsistency. This book hopes to remedy that condition by clarifying and unifying his overall theory, so it can be understood and tested for sociological theory and thinking today. Durkheim produced his groundbreaking treatise, *Suicide*, establishing sociology as a distinctive field of study and demonstrating that social forces are real and can be studied scientifically. He argued that the volume, types, and patterns of suicide are a result of the social forces generated by the moral structure of each society and named these forces integration and regulation. This demonstrated that suicide is not alien to society but instead is a byproduct of the way society is organized. Though his work is over a century old, the problems it confronts, of society's inability to maintain unity and cohesion in the face of increasing diversity, are as relevant today as in Durkheim's time.

By illuminating the contours of Durkheim's famous volume and providing a critical new perspective that shows how its features work, this volume will be an essential resource for sociologists and social theorists of classical and historical sociology, as well as a key volume for courses in sociology of mental health and cultural sociology. It will also serve as an important guide for students and instructors in studying a foundational text and thinker for the discipline.

Bernard B. Berk is Professor Emeritus of Sociology at California State University, Los Angeles. He has taught at a wide range of universities including UCLA, UCSB, University of New Hampshire, CSULA, CSUN, and CSUSD. His areas of specialty include theory, deviance, criminology, penology, and mental illness. He has received numerous teaching awards.

REVISITING DURKHEIM'S SOCIOLOGY OF SUICIDE

A Constructive Framework for Unification and Contemporary Understanding

Bernard B. Berk

Routledge
Taylor & Francis Group
NEW YORK AND LONDON

Designed cover image: Shutterstock

First published 2026
by Routledge
605 Third Avenue, New York, NY 10158

and by Routledge
4 Park Square, Milton Park, Abingdon, Oxon OX14 4RN

Routledge is an imprint of the Taylor & Francis Group, an informa business

British Library Cataloguing-in-Publication Data
A catalogue record for this book is available from the British Library

ISBN: 9781041133346 (hbk)
ISBN: 9781041133339 (pbk)
ISBN: 9781003669272 (ebk)

DOI: 10.4324/9781003669272

Typeset in Sabon
by Newgen Publishing UK

To my most lovable wife who enriches all who know her, Dr. Justin Tillan who made walking possible, and Colin Royston for his editorial assistance and analytical prowess.

CONTENTS

1

INTRODUCTION AND DURKHEIM'S FRAMEWORK

Introduction

Durkheim's study, Suicide, was an important factor in putting sociology on the map and substantially contributed to establishing sociology in academia as a distinctive scientific perspective: Durkheim, over a century ago, produced this groundbreaking treatise, *Suicide* (1897/1952), containing both his research and sociological theory of suicide. *Suicide* (1897) has not only become a classic, but is one of the most, if not the most important, research study in sociology. Many credit Durkheim's trailblazing study with not only establishing sociology as a distinctive field of study but demonstrating that social forces not only exist but can be studied scientifically.

The significance and centrality of *Suicide* (1897) needs little documentation. Scholars describe it as: "one of the greatest pieces of sociological research conducted by anyone" (Merton 1968:63); "the cornerstone of the whole approach taken by most sociologists in the twentieth century" (Douglas 1967:xiii); and "*Suicide* remains a monument" (Pope 1976:204). *Suicide* (1897) is a model of integrating sociological theory and empirical research that has clearly attained the status of an icon in sociology.

Durkheim's study established a connection between the way society is organized and patterns of suicide. This demonstrates suicide *is not alien to society but a byproduct of the way society is organized*. He argued that the volume, types, and patterns of suicide are a result of the social forces generated by the moral structure of each society. These forces act upon individuals from outside themselves, mostly unbeknownst to them, causing them to take their lives.

DOI: 10.4324/9781003669272-1

Suicide (1897) is emblematic of the problems and distresses modern society creates as a result of its changing basis of solidarity and the social forces they create. Suicide is a symptom of the lack of sufficient unifying mechanisms of modern society.

Though *Suicide* (1897) is over a century old, the problems it confronts, of society's inability to maintain unity and cohesion in the face of increasing diversity, are as relevant today as in Durkheim's time.

In his study, Durkheim sets forth basic principles of sociological analysis. One is identifying the interrelationship between the organization of society and individual behavior. He asserts in *Suicide* that as society disintegrates so do the ties that bind individuals to life. As the cohesive forces weaken, individual acts of self-destruction increase. Durkheim's original theory is primarily oriented toward explaining differences among groups in societies' suicide rates; however, it also has implications for predicting individual instances of suicide and may lead to predictions of collective acts of suicide and the total transformation or disintegration of society.

Divergent interpretations of Durkheim's theory have arisen among scholars over the decades reflecting the ongoing interest of scholars in the theory. A problem that has plagued the theory since its inception is the lack of agreement on what Durkheim's theory states and what his study demonstrates.[1]

Numerous interpretations of Durkheim's theory of suicide have emerged over the years among scholars for several reasons. (A) It is *a rich source of fertile ideas*: *Suicide* (1897) is so *richly layered* with insights, that despite a century of scholarship, there remain unexplored areas, unrecognized insights, and unearthed hypotheses in the work. It continues to excite scholars' imaginations in new ways of looking at these issues.

(B) Because *Durkheim did not provide* a single coherent *summary of his theory*, this opened the door to different interpretations arising and left unanswered questions about what all the parts of the theory were, how the parts of the theory fit together, how macro and micro levels of analysis were related, and what specific facts about suicide the theory explains. This also left the door open for scholars to interpret the theory in different ways and sometimes misinterpret the theory.

(C) *Problems in Suicide (1897) also contributed* to its diverse interpretations, ambiguities, and shortcomings in the work resulting from Durkheim's failure to: (i) clearly identify each of the general and specific objectives of *Suicide* and connect them to specific aspects of the theory and relevant supporting evidence, (ii) summarize the overall theory showing how all the parts fit together, (iii) integrate macro and micro levels of analysis tracing the chains of causation and identifying the intervening variables by which macro structures produce individual suicides, (iv) clearly define, operationalize, and measure the key independent variables of integration and regulation, (v) avoid confusing definitional components of integration with its causes and consequences, and using integration to refer to different aspects of social life, like the moral and social structure, (vi) resolve ambiguities and contradictions within the theory, (vii) differentiate the moral from the social structure, identifying their different roles in the chains of causation and as intervening variables in generating suicide, (viii) recognize his theory of egoistic suicide is not a singular theory, but contained multiple explanations of how insufficient integration causes suicide and failing to identify each of the hypotheses and the different social processes and intervening variables they each entail, (ix) specify the various ways social forces cause suicide in the different hypotheses, from creating suicidal impulses, only intensifying already existing impulses, or merely restraining suicidal impulses, and specify their role in each hypothesis, (x) recognize anomie can be caused by other factors than extremes in regulation of appetites, (xi) recognize he changed or lost sight of his original goal of comparing group differences in suicide rates to reveal the nature and relative strength of the social forces creating cohesion, to accounting for the variance in the overall suicide rates, (xii) recognize the independent variables, integration and regulation, were not sufficient by themselves to predict rates of suicide, (xiii) identify many methodological problems using official statistics and questionable data analysis techniques, and (xiv) to connect his theorizing in *Suicide* (1897) to his earlier works like *The Division of Labor* (1893) and *Rules of the Sociological Method* (1895) to show the continuity or change in his thinking, especially in light of arguments that his works must be understood as an interrelated body of theory (Emirbayer 1996) and that his later works depart significantly from his earlier works. These problems throughout *Suicide* will be explored in this text.

(D) *The failure of subsequent research to systematically test and revise the theory also contributes to the lack of clarity, diversity of interpretations, and ongoing disputes within Durkheim's theory.* This lack of rigorous empirical testing did not result in continual revision of the theory, making it more closely aligned with a cumulative body of comparable research findings and current facts about suicide. Since it has not been subject to rigorous empirical testing, unproductive interpretations and unsupported hypotheses have not been discarded or revised to align the theory with the latest research findings, which would help to resolve the conflicts and ambiguities in the theory.

Many studies claiming to be tests of Durkheim's theory are often only tenuously related to the theory and its major concepts. Frequently, they are attempts to fit pre-existing data sets gathered for other purposes to the theory, stretching Durkheim's concepts beyond recognition to fit their data. Nonetheless, they keep ritualistically citing his theory. Thus, both insufficient articulation of the theory and a lack of a cumulative body of knowledge based on rigorous tests of the theory have resulted in *historically inconsistent research findings that have limited sociologists' ability to advance beyond Durkheim's century-old formulations.*[2] Although Durkheim's work remains unsurpassed, an increasing number of scholars have revealed gaps, ambiguities, conflicts, methodological shortcomings, and findings that question Durkheim's theory of suicide (Popora 2015; Stedman-Jones 2013; Gane 1988; Pearce 2001; Pickering and Walford 2000; Lester 1994; Pescosolido and Georgianna 1989; Meštrović 1994 Stack 1980, 2000; Pope 1976; Giddens 1972; Douglas 1967; Johnson 1965; Van Poppel and Day 1996). Others have opened new areas of investigation related to the concerns raised by Durkheim charting new paths (Pescosolido and Georgianna 1989; Bearman 1991; Pescosolido 1986, 1989; Abrutyn and Mueller 2016; 2018; Stack and Kposowa 2008; Wray, Colen, and Pescosolido 2011).

Diversity in Durkheim's sociological contributions have given rise to various interpretations of *Suicide*

Durkheim has contributed a number of paradigms, theories, and sociological methods for studying social life over the course of his career. The following overview explores a range of Durkheim's perspectives, which scholars argue have shifted in focus, method, and theoretical orientation over his career. The diversity of his works has unfortunately caused considerable variation in interpreting Durkheim's theories.

In Durkheim's earliest work, *The Division of Labor*, he proposed structural functionalism as a paradigm for understanding society. Functionalism views society as a social system of interrelated parts where each part contributes to the maintenance of the system, and a change in one part has ramifications for changes in the other parts. The methodology of functionalism is based upon a "part-to-whole analysis," interdependence, and degrees of personal agency rather than causality. Like Darwin, Durkheim views societies adapting to changing environmental conditions and specialization as a response to overpopulation. In this work, Durkheim's primary preoccupation is in social cohesion and what holds society together. In his analysis, he concludes that as societies industrialize, the basic glue that holds society together and the foundation of society, mechanical solidarity, diminishes and is supplanted with a new cohesive force, organic solidarity, that is the result of mutual dependence created by specialization in the division of labor. This gives rise to a central problem in modernity of maintaining cohesion in the face of growing diversity. In addition, a new value in modern society, the cult of the individual, exacerbates the problem of cohesion, as it presents a paradox in uniting modern society by emphasizing the individual over the collectivity.

In his next major work, *The Rules of the Sociological Method* (1895), society's cultural systems are examined. Durkheim sets forth rules for conducting sociological research that entail a new model and paradigm, cultural determinism, which is viewing cultural systems through a scientific lens, as a determinative system following its own laws and determining individuals' behavior (White 1949, 1959). Scientific method will reveal these laws and directions of causality. In this paradigm, individuals are the product of social forces created by society and have no free will, and the direction of influence is from the culture to the individual and not vice versa. Here, we see Durkheim's emphasis as a positivist utilizing the scientific method, proposing laws and identifying the effects of these systems on individual behavior. This paradigm reflects his view that society has an objective reality and can be studied scientifically.

The rules he established for sociologists to study social life were applied in his third major work *Suicide*. In this work, he focuses on how the moral organization, an aspect of culture, gives rise to social forces that cause suicide. This study reflects the application of the scientific method to the problem of weakening social cohesion due to increasing diversity in modern society by viewing suicide as an index of the lack of cohesion. So, suicide is an example of the lack of unification of modern society and how the changing basis of solidarity does not sufficiently attach individuals to preserve their lives and actually creates social forces like egoism that cause them to take their lives. This attempt to create a theory of suicide and laws regulating suicide in society reflects his positivistic methodology measuring the social forces.

His last major work, *Elementary Forms of Religious Life* (1912), scholars regard as a significant departure from his earlier works as it focuses on culture, social meanings, and collective representations. In his study of religion, culture, collective representation, social meanings, symbols, rituals, and collective effervescence all have central importance in his theoretical formulations. He studied early religion as the foundational form for human society as it represented the core of the collective conscience and revealed the fundamental processes creating order, cohesion, and social control in society. A new focus in his methodology is to study the role that social meanings have in creating and maintaining society, focusing on micro-analysis and concern with how people's actions create society and social reality. It is an approach where subjective aspects of social life are more in focus than objective properties of society. Durkheim argues how individuals think and act in the world is determined by categories of thought which were created by religion in earlier times. Categories like time and causality emerge from early religions and continue to be applied in creating social life. Durkheim utilizes the individuals interpreting their life experiences in terms of these social categories promoted by religion as a way of understanding how social life evolves. Thus, his emphasis shifts from objective reality and positivism to subjective reality, social meanings, and interpretive methodology. Collective representations stand for society, and symbols like the flag and the cross are totems that represent society. The central feature of his study and religion is the designation and separation of the sacred from the profane. Objects that acquire sacredness are set apart and protected from the profane. Respect, awe, and extreme punishment set sacred objects apart from all others and signify the power in society embodied in totems, gods, and other symbols that represent society. Sacredness deifies the power of society, achieving greater social control from the awe of sacredness and supernatural forces. Religious rituals not only create cohesion and solidarity but also are performed so intensely that a state of collective effervescence alters the individual's state of consciousness so that life at those moments feel extraordinary and that they are part of something much larger than themselves. The effervescence and altered state of consciousness break down the barriers, so a deeper connection is felt among the members, creating extremely strong bonds and a vision for new possibilities of relating to one another. In addition, they give a new sense of self that is only experienced in society by these rituals (Geertz 1973), which are sometimes intensified by drugs or suspensions of sexual norms. Thus, Durkheim posits two selves, related to the profane and the sacred called homo duplex, where the everyday self emerges from the profane and the heightened self from the collective effervescence. Durkheim examined individual's subjective experiences in society, their identity, and sense of self that emerged from religious rituals, and he argued that the self is on loan to individuals from society.

Although Durkheim's earlier work on societal reactions also focuses on the importance of rituals of exclusion creating social order and solidarity in society, Durkheim fails to cite his work and show how his ideas are related or have changed over time. Therefore, one cannot really conclude whether or not Durkheim abandoned his earlier models because he focused on a different perspective in his later work. Whether Durkheim rejected his earlier works and abandoned them or added an additional dimension based upon his later works is not clear.

In summary, early Durkheim was concerned with social order, how society gains control over individuals, cohesion, and how society maintains solidarity, and these concerns manifest themselves through even Durkheim's later works. In his later works, he focuses more on how societies produce meaning and collective representations through social transformation, collective consciousness, and the evolution of belief systems. Early Durkheim emphasized strict positivist methods. In *Elementary Forms*, he shifts from scientific to interpretive techniques of analyzing social life, seeking not only to understand their functions but also the meaning behind social phenomena. Even when interpretive methods are used to study religion, positivism can be employed by sociologists to test Durkheim's conclusions like 'society worships reifications of itself' (Swanson 1969). Though his methods for studying social life may have shifted, most of his concerns with how societies maintain order, social cohesion, and control over individuals maintain continuity throughout his work. This book will examine whether or not his earlier models have contemporary relevance.

Durkheim's view of sociology provides the framework for *Suicide*

Durkheim defines sociology as the study of society and social forces. His vision of sociology and sociological analysis laid out in *The Rules of the Sociological Method* (1895) provides the basic framework for *Suicide.* Society, and the social forces it generates, are at the center of sociology and his analysis of suicide. Accordingly, Durkheim seeks to identify the social forces that cause suicide and trace their origins in society.

One way he traces their origins is by investigating the differences in rates of suicide between societies, groups and aspects of group life. A second way he traced their origin is by investigating what changes in suicide rates are related to changes in society and group life. For example, he noted an increase in suicide rates as societies industrialized and linked the increase to changes in their moral structure. These changes *both weakened the forces attaching individuals to society and created new forces driving individuals to suicide.*

Durkheim uses "society" to mean different things. One is a process that generates collective representations (Malczewski 2013:170) and another is as a complex structure of connective tissue, and both elements, culture and social structure, ascend as *emergent phenomena with its own distinctive reality.*

Durkheim's functional perspective of society as an interdependent system that is continually evolving or adapting to changing conditions, "becoming" in Stedman-Jones (2013) conception, is articulated in *The Division of Labor in Society* (1893). There Durkheim describes how specialization evolved as a way of populations adapting to the emerging social conditions and how this adaptation transformed the organization of society and basis of solidarity in industrialized societies.

In *Suicide* (1897), he investigated the consequences that the changing basis of solidarity had on attaching individuals to society and regulating their appetites which he hypothesized would be reflected in the changes in rates and patterns of suicide. Though it has been charged that Durkheim lacks an explanation of change, it is clear he employed an evolutionary perspective[3] in the *DLS* (1893) to account for change.

A central preoccupation throughout Durkheim's work is the nature of social cohesion and what holds society together. He was particularly concerned with the causes and consequences of the changing basis of social solidarity in modern society. In *The Division of Labor* (1893), he traces some major consequences of increasing specialization. One especially important consequence is diminishing the collective conscience or the shared moral system of society which is a major source of social cohesion and social control in society.

The collective conscience not only unites society but serves as the foundation or substructure upon which society rests.[4] Specialization weakens this fundamental cohesive force and basic social glue, mechanical solidarity. And were this its sole effect, society would keep disintegrating. However, specialization also gives rise to a new cohesive force, organic solidarity, resulting from the mutual dependence created by specialization.

Durkheim viewed law evolving to protect the sources of solidarity in society. When mechanical solidarity was the sole cohesive force, repressive law pervaded society and sought punishment of violators of the collective conscience to strengthen those norms, as they were the main source of solidarity.

Specialization created mutual dependence and organic solidarity that gave rise to a new form of law, restitutive law, which evolved to protect this new source of solidarity from injury and to repair the system of cooperation, mutual dependence, when damaged.

As the ratio of organic to mechanical solidarity increases in society, the ratio of restitutive to repressive laws also increases and can be taken as an *index of the strength of each source of cohesion*. However, mechanical solidarity remains the foundation on which organic solidarity depends both to ensure that social contracts will be honored and to provide the underlying trust on which beliefs like morality, money, and other unifying systems depend.[5]

Durkheim initially viewed suicide as a negative index of cohesion, though subsequently modified his view, and the increase in suicide a manifestation of the changing basis of solidarity and weakening bonds in modern society. In his study, however, he focused solely on mechanical rather than organic solidarity because organic solidarity was either insufficient or of the wrong character to account for suicide, although later we will demonstrate how his concept of regulation reflected elements of organic solidarity. *It is the moral structure of society that integrates individuals into the social order containing and constraining their behavior that bonds them to society and generates the social forces impelling or failing to restrain individual suicides.* As the collective conscience recedes and group control weakens, individualism, individual freedom, and choice become more widespread creating many of the problems of modernity reflected in *Suicide*.

Another preoccupation running through Durkheim's works, in addition to "what holds society together," is his concern with "how society gains and maintains control over the individual's behavior." This concern is reflected in his analysis of societal reaction theory and how ritual exclusion of some members strengthens the power of society's norms controlling behavior. His study of religion further explored the ways it reinforced society's efforts to control members' behavior and the importance of rituals in intensifying society's influence. He views immersion in the collective conscience as one of the most important ways society controls individual behavior. *Suicide* (1897) furthers that concern as Durkheim attempts to demonstrate the control that moral structures exert over highly personal and idiosyncratic individual behaviors like suicide, as he traces the causes of suicide to the moral tissue of society.

Durkheim believes his theory showed suicide rates were a product of the strength of cohesive and regulatory forces in society generated by its moral structure; both insufficient and excessive degrees of integration and regulation of individuals created high rates of suicide in society.

Integration was a function of the degree to which the moral system was shared and powerful in controlling behavior. Regulation was a function of the moral system's ability to limit individual's aspirations to the opportunities available to achieve individual's goals.

Insufficient integration did not attach individuals sufficiently to society or restrain individual suicidal impulses, and insufficient regulation of aspirations also did not attach individuals sufficiently to society. Both conditions were responsible for the high suicide rates associated with modern society. Excessive integration and overly restrictive regulation of peoples' aspirations or opportunities also resulted in high suicide rates but were more characteristic of pre-industrial societies.

Thus, extremes in the social forces of integration and regulation produced high suicide rates. The forces were generated by the character of the moral system or collective conscience in each society.

Durkheim's study *Suicide* (1897) exemplifies the problems of modernity

Durkheim continues exploring the problems modern societies confront in creating solidarity and social order with a shrinking collective conscience and weakening moral structure that he began investigating in *The Division of Labor* (1893). In *Suicide* (1897), he describes how the weakening moral structure during industrialization increasingly fails to integrate individuals sufficiently into the social order and adequately regulate their behavior and aspirations. This lack of sufficient latticing by the moral structure to contain and constrain individuals contributes to the disintegration of society. It weakens its ability to hold society together and control its members behavior. And by placing individuals more on their own, it increases suicides. Industrialization and increasing specialization are often accompanied by the emergence of consumer capitalism which promotes self-interest that also weakens control by the collective conscience while stimulating unlimited desires for acquisition which also attenuates bonds with society. Furthermore, capitalism generates periodic crises like business cycles and sharp economic fluctuations in modernity. These constitute moral crises creating anomic conditions causing increases in suicides.

This weakening of social controls, increasing self-interest, and unbridled acquisitiveness intensified by periodic crises are symptomatic of problems engendered by modernity. The social forces it unleashes result in increasing suicides manifesting the weakening social ties of advanced societies.

Durkheim's concern with the lack of cohesiveness of modern societies was prescient. Currently, societies and world orders are being torn apart as a result of the absence of sufficient unifying mechanisms, and authoritarian regimes are replacing democracies throughout the world.

Durkheim's objectives in *Suicide*

Durkheim pursues several objectives in *Suicide*. Some were to advance his larger theoretical perspective of the nature of society and social life and others were confined to his research study of suicide.

Objectives related to his larger theoretical concerns of establishing sociology and a general theory of society and social life: Some of these objectives were: (a) to demonstrate that "humans are governed by a higher morality, a collective morality, society" that governs even acts regarded as highly personal, like suicide, (b) to establish that "social behavior is the product of social forces generated by society," by showing patterns of suicide are a product of social forces generated by society, (c) to establish that even "deviance is not alien to society but a byproduct of the way society is organized" by demonstrating both *the volume and forms of suicide are produced by the nature of the moral structure of society and, therefore, a property of society,* and (d) to demonstrate that "suicide is a manifestation of problems engendered by the changing basis of solidarity in modern society" by linking patterns of suicide to changing cohesive forces.

Each of these objectives supports his larger point that society is real and has a powerful impact on people's lives.

Suicide (1897) also reflects some of his broader concerns such as his interest in: (a) how society creates and maintains control over individual's behavior, (b) how the organization of society not only gives rise to patterns of conforming but deviant behavior as well, (c) how the organization of society also generates ideas, beliefs, and sentiments like meaninglessness in his effort to establish a sociology of knowledge elaborated in his study of religion (1912), (d) identifying the social forces that hold society together, and (e) seeking solutions to the problem of unifying modern society reflecting his view of sociology as a tool to solve social problems.

A central preoccupation throughout Durkheim's work, the nature of social cohesion and the social forces that hold society together, is parallel to physicists search for the physical forces that hold matter together.[6] This study also reflects Durkheim's view that sociology is a science that relies on the scientific method to obtain knowledge, and in that sense, Durkheim is a positivist.

Durkheim was more interested in cohesion and the nature of social bonds than in suicide and studied suicide to illuminate the nature of social bonds. Initially, he viewed suicide as a manifestation of the lack of social cohesion and the suicide rate a convenient index of weak social bonds. However, his investigation of altruistic suicide questioned this assumption because suicide could also result from strong social bonds in a group. Whether suicide is a manifestation of weak or strong bonds must be determined by the context and social meaning of the act. One question challenging scholars is whether Durkheim shifted his objective in *Suicide* (1897) from investigating the sources of cohesion, viewing suicide as an index of the lack of cohesion, to accounting for the variance in suicide rates. Did Durkheim lose sight of his original aim, change it during the writing of *Suicide*, or were both objectives pursued? The answer is not clear.[7]

Subsequent research has been mostly oriented toward accounting for variances in suicide rates and scholars criticize these studies for failing to explore the most powerful sources of variance like sex or age on the assumption Durkheim's aim was to account for the variances in suicide rates rather than using differences in suicide rates to identify the causes of social cohesion. If *Suicide* (1897) were judged by the degree of variance it accounts for when compared to gender, for example, it would fall far short of its reputation.[8]

Durkheim's research objectives of his study Suicide (1897): Durkheim had two primary objectives for *Suicide*. The first was to establish that suicide was a social act, and the second was to offer a theory of suicide accounting for differences among societies and groups in suicide rates.

Durkheim's study *Suicide* helped establish sociology in the academic world as a distinctive field of study by showing the fallacy of trying to understand suicide in individual terms. His study demonstrated that the number of suicides with which each society is afflicted is not an aggregate of individual decisions to take their own lives, but rather, the volume of suicides is a distinctive property of each society that requires a sociological explanation to understand. He found that the suicide rates are stable year to year as long as society remains stable. If the suicide rate was a product of individual independent decision making, then the suicide rate would vary depending on the particular individuals in society at that specific period in time. Thus, the rate of suicide would vary as individuals change within society. However, the suicide rate remains the same year-to-year despite the fact that people are continually dying, being born, and aging. If we attribute the suicide rate to the properties of individuals, then it would stand that the rate would vary year-to-year, but the data shows the exact opposite. The turnover is continual, but the suicide rate remains stable as long as society does. This shows that suicide could not be a product of the particular individuals but rather a characteristic of society itself. Further proof is that each society has its own distinctive rate, and when societies change, the rates change in turn. Therefore, this must be a property of society itself. In common sense understandings, suicide can be traced to characteristics of the individuals such as their personality, psychopathology, or experience of tragic events, and thus, motives are sought as the reasons for the suicide. However, Durkheim argues that in some societies no motives are sufficient to cause individuals to take their life as no one has ever done so, and he argues that in other societies almost any motives can trigger suicide. Furthermore, Durkheim argues that social forces which cause people to take their lives are unrecognizable to the people who are affected by them. What Durkheim showed is that it is a property of the society and the state of the cohesive forces that exist that produce the particular volume of suicides with which that society is afflicted. If a sociological explanation is needed to understand this highly personal and idiosyncratic act, then surely it is necessary to understand more widespread patterns of behavior. Something outside of ourselves, that is bigger than ourselves, that is more powerful than ourselves acts upon us shaping our behavior, manifesting the reality and power of society in all aspects of our life. Without a sociological perspective, this phenomena would not be comprehensible. Durkheim's approach has shaped the way sociologists and scholars of suicide have studied suicide for the past 125 years.

Notes

1 Due either to Durkheim's exalted position, richly layered work, incomplete specification, occasional contradiction, or strategic ambiguity, his body of work has become "all things to all people" and like the 60's song, Alice's Restaurant, "you can find anything you want" to justify an interpretation. Many find a phrase or passage in his voluminous works to support a claim that his work reflects a certain approach to sociology they favor, often contradicting other claims. This is also true of his critics, as Stedman-Jones (2001) documents, Durkheim became every school in sociology's boogeyman or arch villain and unfortunately is guilty of the same behavior. This is not hard to do by cherry-picking Durkheim's range of works and sometimes cryptic statements without relating it to the total body of his work or showing how their interpretation applies to his theoretical explanations of a wide variety of social behavior like religion, knowledge, crime, cohesion, ritual, etc. Because the world is infinitely complex with many levels of reality and exceedingly complex inter-connections and can't be grasped in its entirety by any single discipline nor can everything be said at once, various sciences evolved as strategies for abstracting from the complex world. Durkheim grasps at various aspects of the complex social realities and never puts all his work together to reveal the relations among the parts, and there is enough unsaid for interpreters

of his work to render their understandings. Paradigms within sociology serve a somewhat similar purpose in addressing the complex and changing realities. Sociology is not a unified but a multi-paradigmed discipline and fights continually arise in the kitchen over the nature of its subject matter, methods, and the essential problems facing the discipline. Little effort is devoted to fully developing the paradigm and locating specific theories with respect to paradigmatic issues before the action moves on to another way of seeing the world and so Durkheim's place in sociology is continually reassessed. Durkheim, like his unacknowledged disciple Goffman, contributes to the problem by never citing their own works showing how they are connected or if and how he changed his ideas over time.

2 It may be time to stop performing exegeses on Durkheim's texts, divining the holy grail for what Durkheim "really" meant, as though it was a sacred text that would reveal modern truths. Though it has attracted much scholarly attention and opened new avenues of exploration, it has produced few new insights about society or suicide. And after a century of excavating this work with few new avenues for moving the discipline forward, it is time for sociologists to clearly enunciate each plausible interpretation and undertake systematic research evaluating the interpretation's predictive power, and reformulate the theory, for, as Merton states, a discipline that fails to forget its founders is lost. Great literature can open many new ways of looking at the world but scientific theories require explicit and precise propositions.

3 White eloquently applies Durkheim's theoretical approach to understanding social change in his major work, *The Evolution of Culture: The Development of Civilization to the Fall of Rome* (1959). Like Durkheim's analysis in *Suicide*, he focuses on culture, viewing culture as a self-contained system that can be understood without reference to individuals, which follows its own laws, and acts as a powerful force driving society and argues culture should be the central concern of Anthropology. White focused on technology while Durkheim's primary focus in *Suicide* was on a different aspect of culture, the system of moral beliefs, that he believed gave rise to the social forces causing suicide. White's theory soon informed Lenski's (1970) influential theory in sociology of "sociocultural evolution."

4 Harari (2015) asserts that stories, fictions, myths, or similar social constructs form the basis for cooperation among homo sapiens. Society is a mechanism and a system of cooperation by which humans adapt to their environments. Evolution led to a cognitive revolution that permitted symbolling and language that brought forth a new form of thinking and consciousness that supercharged the ways humans can cooperate. This new basis of cooperation transformed sapiens' position on the planet to be a species of significance. Harari believes people agreeing to believe in these fictions is what permits cooperation and group adaptation and can even occur on a world basis since present perils require world cooperation for their solution. Durkheim characterizes such fictions, stories, or myths as part of the collective conscience or moral system and collective understandings which society, and the social forces it generates, imposes on its members. Durkheim seeks to account for the fictions in that the supernatural force they experience is that of society, as power in society becomes centralized and the forces act in a unitary way; reifications of a monotheistic god emerge as people worship this reification of society (Swanson 1969). Another major concern

of Durkheim is how society gains and maintains control over individual behavior and he views religion as supercharging society's authority with a sense of awe and reverence. Durkheim assumes social forces begin influencing people at birth, are always present everywhere shaping their behavior, often outside their awareness. Durkheim is also keenly aware of the social forces of institutions like religion, law, education, kinship, etc. and the informal and formal sanctions in accomplishing those feats. He doesn't focus on the role of force and power in creating or imposing these moralities on members, differentiating specific structures of power or addressing the world order, as his horizon is limited to societies not their inter-relationships. Foucault's (1965, 1975) aim is to reveal the role power and forms of social control like surveillance play in the exercise of power in modern society. Though he, like Durkheim, sees power everywhere and focuses on the role modern institutions play exercising power and monitoring individuals. Whereas Durkheim emphasized the role small size and continual interaction had on group members as ways to maintain constant surveillance and control, Foucault claims modern societies have even more encompassing ways to surveil and control their populations. Harari (2015) advances the analysis seeing modern technology as exponentially enhancing the ability of corporations, government and elites to surveil not only people's movements and actions but even their internal biological states that allow them to understand humans better than they understand themselves. Thus, these corporations can control human behavior, collecting huge amounts of data on them, surveilling all aspects of their lives including biological and emotional monitoring of their internal states, revealing things of which they are even unaware, giving these entities unprecedented ability to manipulate us. He also raises the specter of AI's ability to take control of human lives without being aware of this control. Durkheim would be concerned about modern society's increasing potential for social control and their ability to integrate its members into dystopian social order like Orwell's *1984* where people are brainwashed into accepting its moral regulation and authority so it doesn't chafe and might suggest that suicide is a small price to pay for freedom and the lack of belonging, but as freedom increases, Fromm alerts us to the danger of a rush to totalitarianism and the tribalism it embraces (1969).

5 For example, during the 2008 economic crisis, the economy was on the verge of collapse as banks refused to lend to each other when trust was lost in other bank's solvency, transparency, and ability to repay the daily loans on which the economy depends.

6 Durkheim states, "Collective tendencies have an existence of their own; they are forces as real as cosmic forces, though of another sort... The proof that the reality of collective tendencies is no less than that of cosmic forces is that this reality is demonstrated in the same way, by the uniformity of effects... The important thing is to recognize their reality and conceive of them as a totality of forces which cause us to act from without, like the physico-chemical forces to which we react... They may be measured, their relative sizes compared, as is done with the intensity of electric currents or luminous foci." (1952:273–274) In the same fashion, he examines the impacts of integration and regulation on differences in suicide rates.

7 Douglas (1967:12) cites a shift in Durkheim's use of "integration" as shared meanings in the early chapters to "an equilibrium of opposing forces" (egoism

and altruism) in the later chapters, and Parsons (1949) asserted that Durkheim shifted his objectives in the later chapters.

8 Scheff (2011) estimated Durkheim's theory accounts for 10% of the variance. This is low when compared to variables like gender where males comprise fully 75% of suicides in the U.S. and is even higher in other cultures.

2

DURKHEIM'S THEORY

Establishing suicide as a social act and the identification of the forces causing suicide and their origins

How Durkheim established suicide was socially caused

Durkheim's first step in his study was to establish that suicide, rather than being a highly personal act, was socially caused. To demonstrate this point, he examined suicide rates of various societies and groups for what they might reveal about the causes of suicide.

Durkheim's justifications for believing suicide is socially caused

Non-social causes: Durkheim investigated and rejected non-social causes of suicide concluding suicide must therefore be socially caused. He used two arguments:

a Non-social causes such as insanity, race, climate, etc., could not account for the variations in suicide rates between groups. A flaw in his reasoning, however, was arguing that "if suicides were a function of insanity, they should occur more frequently among groups that had high rates of insanity." Females, therefore, should have higher suicide rates than males because of their higher rates of insanity, yet the opposite was true: suicide is essentially a male phenomenon. So, he concluded that suicide and insanity were unrelated. This error in reasoning, the "ecological fallacy" (Robinson 1950), is drawing conclusions about a relationship between two variables (insanity and suicide) in an individual person based on their statistical relation in an aggregate of persons (a correlation at a group level).

DOI: 10.4324/9781003669272-2

b The second flaw in his reasoning is that his failure to find non-social causes did not prove suicide must be socially caused since he did not examine all possible non-social causes, and the failure to find non-social causes does not prove it is socially caused. His case for social causes, however, rested on more affirmative evidence.

Durkheim's evidence that suicide is socially caused

Social causes: Durkheim argued that *regularities in suicide rates were very strong evidence that suicide was socially caused.* The statistics revealed the following regularities:

1 *Suicide rates for a given society are stable from year to year.* By studying the suicides of a given society as an aggregate whole, Durkheim demonstrated statistically that suicide rates for each of six countries tested varied less from year to year than the respective chief demographic data. From this, he concluded that at each moment of its history, *each society has a definite aptitude for suicide* that is characteristic of that society as long as it remains stable (1952:48).

> "It is not mere metaphor to say of each society that it has a greater or lesser aptitude for suicide...Each group really has a collective inclination for the act, quite its own, and *the source of all individual inclination*, rather than their result. It is made up of the currents of egoism, altruism or anomy running through the society. These tendencies of the whole social body by *affecting individuals cause them to commit suicide*. The private experiences usually thought to be the proximate causes of suicide have only the influence borrowed from the victim's moral predisposition, *itself an echo of the moral state of society*"
>
> *(1952:53) (italics mine)*

Durkheim assumed that these regularities could not be accounted for by regarding suicide as a personal act of violation or despair. For if each individual's unique problems caused them to take their life, irregularity in the suicide rate would be expected due to the variability in individual's emotional states and random variability and fluctuations would occur. The fact that suicide rates remain relatively constant over time despite the turnover in populations, suggests that other factors were at work. It is as though *each society, at a particular point in time, has a fixed quota of suicides*. The regularities cannot be attributed to the characteristics of the members in the society since there is continual turnover in membership as new persons are born and persons continually die while everyone else ages. How could a continually changing population in a society exhibit a relatively stable rate of suicide if that behavior were purely a function of the specific individuals found within the society? Obviously, it must be a property of the stability of society and not of the specific individuals contained within it. And the rate will remain constant as long as the society remains stable.

2 The second fact that established suicide as a social act was that *each society had its own characteristic rate*. Some societies have very high and others very low rates and most fall somewhere in this range. Infants placed at birth in a society where suicide never occurs would be unlikely to ever commit suicide, whereas if they were placed in a society where it was frequent, their risks would accordingly increase. This cannot be explained if one does not take into account that society itself is a prime determinant of suicide.

These two facts were critical in establishing the social nature of suicide. Other facts also supported this conclusion but also pointed to properties of society that seemed to influence the suicide rate.

3 *Each society has its own rate of acceleration in the suicide rate.*

4 *Suicide rates fluctuate with changes in social organization or crises.* When society undergoes a transformation such as industrialization or urbanization, a concomitant change in the suicide rate can also be observed. Passing crises or reorganizations of societies also manifest themselves in the fluctuations in the suicide rates. This generalization supports the notion that the fabric of interrelationships among persons is critical to understanding rates of suicide.

5 *Societies at similar levels of complexity exhibit similar suicide rates.* Industrialized societies tend to have higher suicide rates than non-industrialized societies.

6 *Each sub-group in society has its own characteristic rate of suicide.* Variations in suicide rates are associated with specific subgroups and individual's positions or roles in society.

In short, these statistics reveal the following regularities: (a) each society has a stable rate of suicide despite continual change in its population; (b) each society has its own characteristic rate of suicide; (c) each society has its own rate of acceleration; (d) transformations in social organization or crises in society manifest themselves in fluctuations in rates of suicide; (e) societies at similar levels of civilization exhibit similar suicide rates; and (f) subgroups within society have their own characteristic rates (1952: Book III, Ch. 1).

If suicides were the result of independent individual actions, there would be considerable irregularity in suicide because of the divergent characteristics of persons and, consequently, in the suicide rates of a particular society. Therefore, some extra-individual forces were responsible for the regularities in the suicide rates. Durkheim postulated that *at each moment of its history, each society had a definite, characteristic aptitude for suicide that was a result of the social forces it generated.*

The regularities also suggest: (a) the society, (b) the way its relationships are organized, (c) the intensity of social interaction, and (d) an individual's position or role in society, all play a crucial role in suicide and have to be taken into account in any theory of suicide.

Durkheim did not explore in any depth in *Suicide* (1897) the role of social interaction in suicide other than in intensifying moral forces and in the position or role of individuals in the social structure exposing them to suicidal forces as he focused primarily on the moral structure of society.[1]

These investigations confirmed for Durkheim that:

> The individual is dominated by a moral reality greater than [themselves]; namely, collective reality. When each people is seen to have its own suicide rate, more constant than that of general mortality, that its growth is in accordance with a coefficient of acceleration characteristic of each society; when it appears that the variations through which it passes at different times of the day, month, and year, merely reflect the rhythms of social life; and that marriage, divorce, the family, religious society, the army, etc., affect it in accordance with definite laws, some of which may even be numerically expressed—these states and institutions will no longer be regarded simply as characterless, ineffective, ideological arrangements. Rather *they will be felt to be real, living, active forces which, because of the way they determine the individual, prove their independence of [them].*
> *(1952:xxxvii)*

Durkheim believed these facts proved that suicide was a social phenomenon related to the character of the society which "At each moment of its history, therefore, each society has a definite aptitude for suicide" (1952:xlv). This regularity in suicide rates and their increases impressed Durkheim as the stuff of natural sciences (Douglas, 1967:9). He assumed these regularities could not be the result of free will of individuals, but that some extra-individual factor determined the wills of individuals in the society. If free will were determining actions of others, then there could only be gross irregularity in suicide rates (Douglas, 1967:9). After Durkheim established suicide as socially caused, he stated that the central problem for sociologists is to account for the volume of suicides with which each society is afflicted at a specific moment in time. This led to his second objective to formulate a theory that could account for the variance in rates of suicide between different groups and societies.

Durkheim's second goal in *Suicide*: Proposing a theory of suicide

Believing he had established suicide rates were socially caused and a property of the society, his next step was to propose a theory to account for differences in the suicide rates between groups and shifted his focus to identifying the social forces in society responsible for suicides. By analyzing and understanding the social causes of suicide, he hoped his theory would reveal what held society together. His theory of suicide had three goals: (a) to identify the nature of the social causes of suicide; (b) to show how these causes produce their effects, and (c) to identify the relation of social causes to individual acts of suicide[2] (1952:li).

Several influences may have shaped his construction of the theory. First was his effort in *The Division of Labor* where he had already identified two causes of social cohesion, mechanical and organic solidarity. The second influence may have evolved from his efforts in proving suicide was socially caused. The third stream of influence evolved from his analysis of religious differences, group membership, and size of the group on suicide rates where he was exploring the role of moral beliefs in creating cohesion.

Durkheim's broader concern was understanding the nature of social cohesion and social bonds in society, and suicide was of interest because it constitutes the severing of bonds with society. Investigating suicide might then reveal the processes that bond individuals to one another and to society.

Durkheim had already identified two major sources of cohesion unifying society and bonding individuals to society (1933): (a) mechanical solidarity, created by strongly held shared moral beliefs and practices governing individuals' behavior, and (b) organic solidarity created by the interdependence fostered by specialization in the division of labor in society. In *Suicide* (1897), it is often believed that Durkheim focused exclusively on mechanical solidarity which he viewed as the *fundamental cohesive force in all societies, including modern societies.*[3] Along with mechanical solidarity or integration, Durkheim identified a second social force causing suicide which he labeled "regulation." Both were cohesive forces associated with bonding individuals to society and contributed to suicide.

Many believe he also disregarded any role organic solidarity might play in suicide, although he briefly discussed the role occupational groups might play in creating solidarity in modern society (1952:1–31).

In the *DLS* (1893), Durkheim focused on what he regarded as the primary consequence of specialization, creating structural differentiation which reduced the sphere of the collective conscience decreasing mechanical solidarity. In *Suicide* (1897), he explored in more depth *the effects of decreasing mechanical solidarity which were (a) weakening the forces attaching individuals to society, and (b) unleashing a new social force, egoism, causing increased suicides* in modern society. Another consequence of increasing industrialization and capitalism is anomie which also weakens peoples' attachment to society and creates sentiments driving individuals to suicide.

Initially, Durkheim viewed suicide as a manifestation of the lack of social cohesion and suicide rates as a negative index of cohesive forces since suicide represented extreme withdrawal from society. His analysis of altruistic suicide led to questioning the purity of suicide as an index of negative cohesion. By investigating the forces that weaken social bonds, he believed, the basis of social cohesion could be clarified. In the *DLS* (1893), two cohesive forces, mechanical and organic solidarity were identified, and in *Suicide* (1897), he sought to advance his investigations of cohesion and social bonds by identifying a new force, regulation, and measuring the strength of social forces like mechanical solidarity utilizing the suicide rate as a negative index of its presence and of the overall solidarity of society.[4]

The first phase of his study established that suicide was socially caused and that the patterns of suicide were a property of the way society was organized. Durkheim was led to the conclusion that suicide was a social phenomenon because each society manifested a stable rate of suicide, and each had its own distinctive rate of suicide and rate of acceleration along with other statistical regularities that supported the conclusion that suicide was socially caused.

When analyzing this evidence, he implicitly left the impression that his theory would account for the volume or rate of suicides with which each society was afflicted. He regarded this fact about suicide as the central problem addressing sociologists, but this problem was ultimately left unfulfilled in *Suicide* (1897). It is unclear whether he gave up on that objective because he recognized his theory could not account for those facts, lost sight of his original goal, or changed his objectives in the later part of *Suicide*. In any case, he settled on a lesser goal of accounting for why one group or society had a higher rate than another in place of accounting for the volume of suicides with which each society was afflicted. Durkheim strongly believed that suicide statistics reflect the suicidal tendency with which each society is afflicted, and his analysis creatively pursued statistical associations which he hoped would unlock the key to the social causes since these differences could only be accounted for by differences in the character of group life.

Since Durkheim believed social forces cause all social behavior and are at the root of all sociological investigation, it is only natural he sought to identify the social forces that produced suicides.

The second phase in his study and the beginning of the construction of his theory sought to identify the social forces that are responsible for the differences in suicide rates between groups and societies. He would proceed to explain how these social forces cause suicide after he identified them.

Durkheim's theory continued: The two social forces causing suicide – integration and regulation

Durkheim traced the roots of suicide to two social forces, described as integration and regulation, which work in different ways to attach or detach individuals from society. Strengthening or weakening the forces attaching individuals to society will impact the volume/rate and types of suicides in each society.

Descriptions of the forces:

Integration is a social force characterizing *how thoroughly society controls people's behavior by its system of morals. A highly integrated society would have a powerful system of shared moral beliefs that governs extensive areas of individuals' lives.*

Regulation characterizes *the degree to which the moral system regulates individual's social appetites or aspirations, so they are in balance with what is realistically attainable in their social circumstances motivating individuals to keep pursuing their social existences.* A society is well regulated when that society limits individuals' aspirations to what is attainable, so people are sufficiently motivated to pursue social goals and are subsequently bonded to society.

Types of suicide: The two social forces form the basic framework of his theory. From these two forces, Durkheim derived four types of suicide. Each type represents extreme positions on the dimensions of integration and regulation.

Egoistic suicide results from a low degree of integration while *altruistic* suicides from a high degree of integration. *Anomic* suicides result from a lack of regulation and *fatalistic* suicides from an overabundance of regulation. This characterization of Durkheim's theory turned out to be overly simplistic with further investigation which will be addressed later. Each type of suicide is caused by different social processes emanating from the different social conditions that give rise to them.

Differences in strengths and types of forces account for differences in the rates and types of suicide

Durkheim's theory hypothesizes that the two social forces, integration and regulation, account for the differences in rates and types of suicide between societies. He had already concluded in the *DLS* (1893) that the fundamental cohesive force bonding individuals to society was mechanical solidarity and labeled this force integration in *Suicide* (1897).

This system of shared beliefs united groups, attached individuals to society, and integrated them into the social order. Both forces, integration and regulation perform cohesive functions, attaching individuals to society, but operate on different principles.

Durkheim's theory continued: The origins of social forces

Durkheim's objective for his theory was to identify the social causes, show how each causes suicide, and trace the origin of the forces causing suicide in society. Durkheim believed the two forces, integration and regulation, were generated by and emanated from the character of the moral structure or collective conscience of society. He viewed the collective conscience as the foundation of society which creates social order, unifies society, and is central to society's gaining control over member's behavior. Integration is a measure of the degree to which the moral system or collective conscience controls the individual's behavior. Highly integrated societies are those whose moral system *is widely shared, strongly held, effectively controls conduct over extensive areas of social life, and secures individuals tightly to the social order*. The degree to which the moral structure contains and constrains individuals reflects its degree of integration. To the extent the number of shared beliefs is diminished, less strongly held, or their power to regulate conduct is weakened or controls fewer areas in life, integration is weakened.

Regulation refers to the degree to which the moral structure, after social desires motivating people to pursue cultural goals are instilled in members, restrains their appetites and desires *to the level where they are sufficiently satisfied to continue pursuing their lives and social existences*. When restraints over desires are weakened creating an abundance of unsatisfied desires with the consequence of unbearable frustration, or when desires are so thwarted at every turn that it equally results in unbearable frustration and hopelessness, the will to live and bond to society is weakened and these pressures make them vulnerable to suicide. To the extent that regulation is either too lax or extreme, the society is poorly regulated and will manifest high suicide rates. The underlying notion is that a certain level of satisfaction of one's socially created desires or appetites is necessary to sustain one's motivation to continue living. The force of regulation is a function of the moral structure (goals) and its relation to the social structure providing sufficient opportunities to attain those goals.

A highly integrated society creates sufficient forces to produce social order and cohesion, binding people together and strongly adhering them to society. Integration, therefore, refers to the degree to which the moral structure controls the individual's actions, thereby attaching them to society. Regulation refers to *the degree to which the moral structure regulates aspirations to be in balance with what is realistically attainable in their social conditions, making life sufficiently satisfying to pursue a social existence.*

The problems created by modern society impair both its ability to integrate members sufficiently into society and regulate their aspirations appropriately to their circumstances that result in increasing suicide rates.

In the transition from an agricultural to an industrial society, Durkheim describes the inevitable erosion of the collective conscience as a result of specialization, and consequently, this decline of mechanical solidarity weakens society's ability to integrate individuals into the social order, throwing them more on their own and thus increasing suicides.

Often accompanying the rise of industrialization is consumer capitalism. This fuels materialism and unquenchable desires, giving rise to excessive hopes reflecting the deregulation increasing anomic suicide. In addition, capitalism is also fueling self-interest fostering egoism and disruptive business cycles, rapid expansions, sharp declines, and periodic crises, which alter the balance between aspirations and opportunities creating anomic conditions and suicides.

Rapid social change is yet another condition that creates deregulation and insufficient guidelines where new norms regulating aspirations and expectations have not yet evolved.

In integration, it is the control by the moral structure that attaches individuals to society and in insufficiently integrated societies prevents them from taking their life or in highly integrated societies commands them to forfeit their life. In regulation, it is the level of gratification of socially created desires that are possible in their social circumstances that attaches individuals to society or detaches them from society in anomic or fatalistic suicides. Changes in values like increasing materialism, self-interest, or excessive desire alter the moral structure of society creating anomic pressures.

Evidence Durkheim relied upon to support his interpretations: Since the collective conscience or moral structure is the basic source of mechanical solidarity and cohesion, Durkheim pointed to the shrinking collective conscience during industrialization as key to the decline of cohesion. In *Suicide* (1897), he also cited the decline of common morality and practices giving rise to the spirit of free inquiry which were responsible for the religious differences in suicide rates. He also cited the lack of control by a common morality of individuals who lacked group membership such as the single or divorced persons who have higher suicide rates than married persons. He pointed out that the power of group morality increased with the size of the family which increased dynamic density so that larger families had lower rates of suicide, and in comparison, divorced individuals freer of group constraints had higher rates of suicide. The higher rate of suicide among the educated, who were less governed by tradition and religion, supported his belief that the weakening power of the moral structure created suicides. He also could have pointed to the fact that increasing suicides are correlated with other forms of non-conformity like crime, alcoholism, addiction, etc. This is due to the fact that modern society has weaker social control over most behavior in comparison to earlier forms of society. These relationships were sufficient for Durkheim to believe that the force of integration declined and produced more suicide as a result of changes in the moral structure of society.

His efforts to link the force of regulation to the moral structure were both less explicit and less extensive. The moral structure contains the cultural goals to which people aspire, the rules by which the goals could be appropriately attained, and the levels of rewards appropriate to each status in society. He cited statistical relationships between business cycles and suicide rates to support his claims but did not elaborate the chain of causation between economic fluctuation and suicide rates or the intervening variables responsible for the relationship. He also did not elaborate these connections for periods of rapid social change or rising capitalism.

Durkheim pursued identifying social causes by examining the statistical regularities believing they would reveal the underlying social causes and addressed how each of the forces produces suicides in the various chapters on the different types of suicide.

Notes

1 This lack of clarity of the roles of the moral system versus the social structure and social interaction in creating suicide needs further investigation since Durkheim also introduced levels of social interaction to his explanation of seasonal variations in the suicide rates, social density in the size of families, and later in the text also cited both social isolation and group support as intervening variables in the links between low integration and egoistic suicide which are aspects of social organization and social structure not moral structures of society. The social structure and social context were also intimately involved in anomic and fatalistic suicide as factors limiting the attainment of goals, such as the availability of potential mates due to large casualties during war.

2 It is clear from these three stated objectives that Durkheim did not intend to account for either the volume of suicides or variances in suicide rates, and he had an interest in linking social causes to individual suicidal acts.

3 Durkheim never identifies the processes by which regulation bonds people to society, sufficiently gratifying member's social appetites, as either mechanical, organic, or yet a third source of cohesion.

4 Earlier (1933) Durkheim suggested the ratio of repressive to restitutive law could be used as an index of the contribution of mechanical to organic solidarity to the overall cohesiveness of society but made no attempt to measure the strength of mechanical and organic solidarity in this fashion.

3

HOW THE SOCIAL FORCES CAUSE DISTINCTIVE TYPES OF SUICIDE

Durkheim's theory continued: The four types of suicide – Egoistic

Identification of the first social cause – egoism: Durkheim sought to identify the types of suicide based on *the similarity of their causes*. "Egoistic" suicides resulted from the weakening of the group's control over the individual's behavior.

> The more weakened the groups to which he belongs, the less he depends on them, the more he consequently depends only on himself and recognizes no other rules of conduct than what are founded on his private interests. . . . egoism [is when] the individual ego asserts itself to excess in the face of the social ego and at its expense, we may call egoistic the special type of suicide springing from excessive individualism.
>
> *(1952:167–168)*

Durkheim relied on earlier studies to identify regularities in the suicide rates. Only regularities would reflect the social forces at work and allow him to separate social causes from idiosyncratic suicidal acts. After exploring differences in suicide rates between different religious confessions, marital conditions, and states of the polity, Durkheim concluded that the differences could be explained by the degree of integration of the various groups. Low levels of integration were associated with high rates of "egoistic" suicide. The social law was accordingly stated: "suicide varies inversely with the degree of integration of the group" (1952:167).

Religious Societies: Durkheim began his investigation with religious societies which revealed significant differences between religious

DOI: 10.4324/9781003669272-3

groups: Protestants had higher suicide rates than Catholics, who, in turn had higher suicide rates than Jews. What explanation could be offered for these differences?[1] Durkheim rejected the notion that the lower suicide rate of Catholics resulted from the stronger sanctions Catholics imposed upon suicide, because Jews were the least likely to punish suicide, yet had the lowest suicide rate. Durkheim argued that the essential difference between Catholicism and Protestantism was that Protestantism permitted far greater free inquiry than Catholicism. Catholicism sought total control over the individual's conscience and offered a faith that was ready-made and which could be taken over without scrutiny. The Catholic religion, organized into a hierarchical system of authority, served to render tradition invariable since all variation is abhorrent to Catholic thought. Whereas in Protestantism, the Bible is put into the hands of worshipers and no interpretation is imposed upon them. The very structure of Protestantism stresses religious individualism. Only in England was the Protestant clergy organized into a hierarchy. Furthermore, in Protestantism, ministers, like worshipers, have no other source of guidance but their selves and their consciences. Therefore, Durkheim concluded, the proclivity of Protestants toward suicide must relate to this *spirit of free inquiry*. Free inquiry results from Protestants having fewer common beliefs and practices than Catholics. Protestants were freed more from the yoke of tradition than Catholics.

How integration binds people to groups: Common beliefs weld members together and unite groups. Durkheim's concepts of the "collective conscience" and "mechanical solidarity" were based upon the assumption that cohesion resulted from sharing common norms, beliefs, and rituals. The larger the scope of these common beliefs, the more potent the normative system's regulation of the individual's behavior is. The greater the individual judgment the religion permits, the less it tends to dominate lives, and the less its cohesion and vitality will be developed, and the fewer strings will exist to tie the individual to the group by virtue of their common loyalty. Hence Durkheim concludes that Protestants are less strongly integrated as a religious body than Catholics. By "integration" Durkheim refers to "common beliefs and practices." Adherence and conformity are the hallmarks of a strongly integrated group, whereas reflection and discussion of those of a loosely integrated group.

Jews were also a highly integrated group but for different reasons. Oppression forced the Jews to form strict unions among themselves. Each community became a compact society with strong feelings of self-consciousness and a coherent body. Everyone thought and lived alike, which had the effect of reducing individual differences and providing a common core of values, norms, and practices. This was precisely what Durkheim meant by integration. Both Catholicism and Judaism leave little room for individual variation.

Having formulated a hypothesis linking "integration and suicide" on the basis of the differences between religious groups, Durkheim sought to test his hypothesis by examining further differences among groups.

The evidence in support of egoistic suicide

Supporting evidence for the inverse relation hypothesis: Durkheim's first test of the hypothesis was to examine the differences in integration between various protestant sects. The Church of England was a more integrated Protestant sect than others; therefore, he argued that it should exhibit a lower suicide rate than other Protestant sects. The data supported his hypothesis. A second test explored the effect of education. Knowledge, he argued, frees one from the yolk of tradition and reflects a weakening of collective sentiments over the individual. People seek both to learn and to kill themselves because of the loss of cohesion of religious society; a state of moral individualism prevails. The more numerous and strong these collective beliefs are, the stronger the integration and the greater its preservative value upon the individual's life. Higher rates of suicide were therefore predicted as the amount of education increased. These differences were also supported by the data. Third, other groups, he reasoned, must have the same effect. Persons who were integrated into groups should have lower suicide rates than those who were isolated, and he found married males had a lower suicide rate than single males, but single females did not. Marriages that produced children decreased suicide for both sexes. The size of the family was related to the degree of integration because collective sentiments are strengthened by continual interaction among members which provide continual reinforcement of the norms giving them strength and vitality. No powerful traditions, which unite members in a group, persist in small families, which are most commonly tied by the feelings of the members for each other. In this sense, small families do not have an existence outside the immediate members' lives. His data indicated that as the size of the family increased, suicide decreased.[2] Fourth, if minority status increases cohesion, then in countries where Catholics were a minority, their suicide rates should be lower than where they are a majority. This was also confirmed by Durkheim's investigations. His fifth test proposed suicide is more likely in a disintegrating society than one that is highly integrated. During periods of crises or war when society is more united, the suicide rate should decrease, and it does. These tests established for Durkheim, that the more strongly constituted (integrated) the group, the stronger the safeguards against suicide. Durkheim concluded that the significant character of religion, family, and political groups are that they are strongly integrated groups, and he formulated the hypothesis that: *suicide varies inversely with the degree of integration of the group*.

The cause of egoistic suicide, therefore, can be traced to the moral tissue of society, specifically in its normative structure of common beliefs and practices, which both controls individuals' behavior and creates social cohesion. As the group disintegrates, the individual detaches themself from social life. As they become less dependent on the group, they come to recognize no other rules of conduct other than those founded on their private interests. Under those circumstances, the individual ego asserts itself to excess in the face of the social ego and at its expense. *Egoistic suicide springs from excessive individuation caused by the lack of integration*. Durkheim is asserting that it is society's loss of control over individuals that allows them to do what society ordinarily prohibits, take their life, except in certain circumstances in altruistic societies where society requires self-sacrifice.

Thus, as society disintegrates and the moral system atrophies, both (a) the weakening of social forces restraining individuals with suicidal impulses and (b) the emergence of new social forces causing sentiments of meaninglessness and purposelessness impelling individuals towards suicide generates a specific volume of egoistic suicides in each society or group.

Numerous conditions can induce individuals to want to take their lives, but society ordinarily prohibits such behavior. Durkheim says little about the origins of suicidal impulses other than that society creates some like sentiments of meaninglessness or purposelessness or "life is not worthwhile or futile" in the process of its disintegration. As society disintegrates its ability to restrain suicidal behavior, from whatever sources, diminishes and it creates new suicidal pressure which gives rise to the particular suicide rate the society exhibits. The stream of suicidal behavior is comprised of those who are suicidal directly from the disintegration of society and those whose source is not from the disintegration of society but unspecified, minus the strength of society's remaining moral system to restrain people from acting on their suicidal impulses from all sources. *It is society's failure to control the individual's behavior that permits egoistic suicide*. Durkheim is not able to determine what percent of the suicides result from its failure to restrain individuals adequately and what percent of those motivated to take their life are a result of egoistic forces in society. Thus, egoism causes suicide in two ways: (a) a failure to restrain suicidal impulses, and (b) the emergence of sentiments as society disintegrates generating feelings of meaninglessness and purposelessness that cause people to end their life.

The central factor causing egoistic suicide, therefore, is the lack of sufficient integration in society, shared values, norms, beliefs, and practices in the group, which both fail to restrain individual's suicidal impulses and create suicidal impulses as society disintegrates. One source of ambiguity and misunderstanding of Durkheim's theory of suicide is not elaborating the different ways egoistic suicide occurs, which will be examined next.

Durkheim's theory: The second type of suicide – Altruistic

Durkheim found suicide also occurred in highly cohesive societies, *but for different reasons, and concluded not all suicides were the product of the lack of attachment to society.* He formulated the concept of altruistic suicide, which resulted from *high degrees of integration.* Just as excessive individuation can cause suicide, so can insufficient individuation. Altruistic suicides were examples of moral understandings giving rise to *social forces compelling or extolling suicide* and individual's very strong attachments to society created little resistance in them to conforming to those social expectations.

"When man has become detached from society, he encounters less resistance to suicide in himself, and he does so likewise when integration is too strong." (1952:175). The source of resistance to suicide within individuals is the degree to which society exercises control over them. The less it does, the more individuals feel free to disregard their obligations. In the most common manifestation of egoistic suicide, society has loosened its grip over the individual sufficiently to permit them to feel that they have the right to take their life even though it may conflict with their obligations to society. The other cause of egoistic suicide results when collective sentiments of meaninglessness and purposelessness evolve, impelling individuals to feel their lives are not worth living and acting upon those sentiments. *These collective sentiments result from society's disintegration, but the individual's actions are still being impacted by societal forces and are similar to altruistic suicides. It is society's presence that pushes individuals toward suicide.* The negative evaluations of life reflect the disintegration of society and its moral structure. Altruistic suicides also reflect societies' bidding, but not necessarily from a negative evaluation of life due to its disintegration. Thus, altruistic suicide results from different social forces, excessive integration, and involves different social processes and intervening variables.

In cohesive societies, individuals do not kill themselves because they assume the right to, as in egoistic suicide, but because it is their duty. If they fail in this obligation, they are dishonored or punished. The weight of society is brought to bear upon the person to destroy themself. The role of society in the two types of suicide is somewhat different. Society intervenes in egoistic suicide by forbidding the choice of death. Whereas, in altruistic suicide, it speaks of a sentence of death. It is a question of to whom one's life belongs, society or the individual. Hence the "taking" of one's life in egoistic suicide is "from" society, and in altruistic suicide, it is most often "for" society. Traditional and modern societies have different answers to the question of "whose life is it, anyway?"

For society to be able to compel its members to kill themselves, the individual personality can have little value. For the individual to occupy so little place, they must be completely absorbed in the group. This can only be accomplished in a highly cohesive society. The right to an individual personality and personal inclinations is not conceded strongly by a highly cohesive society.[3]

In a highly cohesive group, the individual's life is rigorously governed by custom and habit. Everyone leads the same life, exhibits the same ideas, values, and shares common occupations and outlooks. Because of its small size, the group is close to everyone and loses no one from sight. Collective supervision is constant, extending to almost every area of life.[4] The individual cannot set up his or her own environment and thereby forges a uniqueness that is the basis of individuation. They are only a part of a whole, and for other parts to have so little life of their own, the whole must be the center of gravity of social attention. Indistinct from companions, they have little value apart from the whole. As such intense identification develops, the individual does not come to distinguish between their interests and those of the group. This individual life is valued so little that it can be easily dispensed with by the group and individual.

Thus, whereas egoistic suicide occurs because of excessive individuation, altruistic suicide is a result of insufficient individuation. Egoistic suicide occurs because society allows individuals to escape it; altruistic suicide occurs because society holds too strict a tutelage on the individual and may require it. Egoism refers to a state where ego is living its life and obeying itself alone; altruism is the opposite state where ego is not its own property, and the goal of conduct is exterior to itself: the group's goals are paramount.

Altruistic suicide is a duty, albeit with differing degrees of obligatoriness attached to it. (a) *Obligatory suicide* occurs when the norms require it. Failure to conform, results in punishment and dishonor. (b) *Optional suicide* is when public opinion does not formally regulate it but is favorable to the act and social prestige is attached. In optional suicide, the act is done to win esteem. In both cases the individual is trained in renunciation and unquestioning acceptance of the group. (c) *Joy of sacrifice* occurs where renunciation of life is considered praiseworthy, and goals outside of life seem more real and important. Suicide bombers exemplify this pattern. Another type that might be considered as a form of altruistic suicide not described by Durkheim is that resulting from: (d) *Group rejection* or the lack of social acceptance. When the group is the center of the individual's social existence and defines their core identity, the lack of its acceptance denies the individual their all and the basis of their existence. Group condemnation is tantamount to self-condemnation if the group is all that matters. The individual who commits suicide could also be seen as ridding the group of a despised person, as condemnation by others leads to self-hatred.

In egoistic societies, the individual is given the highest social value with little subordination to the group. In altruistic societies, individuals are given little value and are totally subordinate to the group.

There are some special environments sometimes in even loosely integrated societies, such as the military, where altruistic suicide is chronic. The soldier, trained to put little value on their life, to sacrifice life, and to obey without question or even understanding, is trained in altruism. Soldiers may prefer death to defeat or personal disgrace and set little store on their life compared to their duty. The least disappointment such as a reprimand, insult, or punishment can lead to desperate resolutions. Where the group is all, the loss of group acceptance results in the loss of all one's worth.[5]

Thus either: (a) because the norms require or favor it, or (b) because of a failure to meet group expectations or experiencing social rejection, the individual will forfeit their life. Because there is such a fusion with the group, group condemnation is tantamount to self-condemnation. If the individual's self-respect is tied to one group, then when it is withdrawn, they have no further basis for self-esteem. The act of suicide in cohesive societies is a socially approved way of conforming, winning esteem, restoring a fall from grace, or ridding the group of a despised person.

Comparison of egoistic and altruistic suicide

Egoistic suicide is an example of the individual asserting their interest above social interests and therefore is a violation of social expectations and duties. Whereas altruistic suicide is an example of conforming to group standards and manifestation of strong group pressures to conform, egoistic suicide, resulting from the pressures of collective sentiments of meaninglessness imposed on individuals causing suicide, is similar to the process by which altruistic suicide occurs and reflects conformity to social sentiments but occurs in less strongly integrated groups and the sentiments echo the group's disintegration.

Both egoistic and altruistic suicide are symptomatic of the ways individuals are integrated into society. Egoism results from inadequate integration and altruism from over integration into society. Both represent extremes in social integration but involve very different social processes in achieving their effects.

The degree of integration in society is a function of the degree of individuation of members within the group. High individuation leads to egoism were the individual ego asserts itself to excess in the face of the social ego and at its expense. Egoistic suicide springs from excessive individualism where a reduced lack of social concerns exists. The individual loses sight of the group and overemphasizes his or her own ego as they become estranged from the group. Egoism is under identified with group goals while altruism reflects an over identification with group goals.[6]

People who experience social rejection are more at risk for suicide in both loosely and highly integrated societies. In highly integrated societies, the effects of social rejection may be more severe as the uniformity of the rejection is greater than in loosely integrated societies and such traditional cultures change more slowly. In the U.S., lesbian and gay teenagers had high rates of suicide but as a result of pride movements, they have achieved more acceptance and the expectation would be the suicide rates should decrease due to increased social acceptance and increase again with new attacks on their rights. The increase in suicides is currently among teens during the pandemic, when young people are disconnected from school and friends. This results from the disintegration of their social networks, reflecting egoistic suicide, but is linked to the shutting down of social interaction not to changes in the moral systems.

There were significant differences in the approach and evidence supporting his assertions in his analysis of egoistic and altruistic suicide. Within his section on egoistic suicide, Durkheim integrated theory and research findings, comparing differences in suicide rates among religious groups. This integration of theory and research was absent in his analysis of altruistic suicide, relying mostly on broad examples without statistical comparisons except for military-civilian comparisons. This difference in approach continues through Durkheim's analysis of anomic and fatalistic suicide.

Now, we will address the second primary force causing anomic and fatalistic suicide, regulation.

Durkheim's theory: A second force and third type of suicide – Anomic

Durkheim observed the effects of a second social force, in addition to integration, causing suicide in other regularities in the suicide rates. Durkheim did not elaborate the formulation of each of the steps in his theory of anomie nor did he integrate it with supportive facts comparing suicide rates as he had in his theory of integration and egoistic suicide. He found earlier advanced societies and implied capitalistic societies had even higher suicide rates than other modern societies. Modern societies had high rates of suicide due to the decline of integration resulting from increased specialization in the division of labor during industrialization. These higher rates in advanced and capitalistic societies indicated to him the presence of a second independent social force causing suicide that he labeled regulation. To reiterate, regulation characterizes the degree to which the moral system regulates individuals' social appetites or aspirations, so they are in balance with what is realistically attainable in their social circumstances.

Another set of facts that also supported his claim of the existence of a second force was the increases in suicide rates during particular time periods within a society. For example, they increased during economic fluctuations. He also identified crises and periods of rapid social change as other times that also increased suicides but presented no data in support of these assertions.

After he believed he established the existence of this second force, he proceeded to describe how it caused suicide. The main fact that alerted Durkheim to this force was that as societies became prosperous or developed capitalism, suicide rates increased even more in comparison to other industrialized societies.

Durkheim then explained how these conditions led those societies to have higher suicide rates. As societies became prosperous or developed capitalism, materialism and unlimited acquisition of wealth emerged as cultural values. Durkheim believed *these values contributed to further increases in suicide rates than declining integration was responsible for in modern society.* Durkheim never presented data to support his case of an independent effect on the overall suicide rate. Nonetheless, he proceeded, arguing that as societies unfolded with those values, suicide rates increased rapidly to alarming proportions.

With respect to integration, what increased suicide rates in modern society was the lack of common values that bonded individuals to society. Whereas, with respect to this second force, regulation, the emergence of materialism and unlimited acquisition as values created frustration and dissatisfaction with one's lot in life, weakening the bond with society and also increasing the suicide rates in modern society. Other conditions like economic fluctuations, crises, and periods of rapid social change produced the same effects.

How materialism and unlimited acquisition gave rise to increases in the suicide rates: These values create unquenchable appetites in the members of those societies so that no matter how much individuals acquired, they were never satisfied and always wanted more.

Durkheim asserted that without sufficient restrains on those appetites, individuals will experience more and more frustration until it becomes unbearable and the anger it generates will be turned inward in self-annihilation. Hence, Durkheim gave the label regulation to the second social force that bonded individuals to society and whose excesses cause suicide. This conclusion runs parallel to his explanation and connection of integration and egoistic suicide. Similarly, unquenchable appetites are a major contributor to suicides caused by this second force, regulation, in modern societies.

He examines in more depth how the cultural values of materialism and unlimited acquisition create problems and cause suicide. He states that each society creates in individuals social appetites. Individuals are not born with desires to work, marry, be moral, or respected. They are born with certain biological requirements or needs like hunger and thirst. Many of these biologically based appetites have built-in regulatory mechanisms or satiation points that signal to the individual when they have eaten or drunk enough. These mechanisms regulate the individual's appetite and signal when they are temporarily sated or satisfied.

However, this is not the case for social appetites. Some external force is necessary to limit these appetites. Durkheim argues society must set these limits. If they fail to set limits, individuals will continually desire more and more, feeling perpetually dissatisfied that they never have enough. Feeling they never have enough and always desiring more generates frustration, anger, and sometimes rage that provide the motivation for individuals to take their lives.

Durkheim states that unchecked desire can only be a source of torment. If the individual's needs require more than can be granted, there will be continual friction, and the individual can only function painfully. Actions that are painful are soon discontinued as unsatisfied tendencies atrophy. Since the desire to live is, in part, dependent on the balance of actions to bring sufficient rewards to make living tolerable, insufficient fulfillment of rewards would lead toward the individual taking their life.

Social desires, unless checked, are by their nature limitless. Therefore, some external restraint must be imposed to stave off what might be continual frustration. Individuals must not feel all their efforts are in vain, and that by walking they have advanced. One does not advance, however, if the goals are unclear, infinite, or limitless. To pursue a goal which is unattainable is to condemn oneself to perpetual unhappiness. Hope cannot survive repeated disappointments and if the future can offer no more than the past, it is not a pleasant prospect. The more one has, the more one wants, since satisfaction will only stimulate one's needs instead of fulfilling them.

The only thing that can regulate human desire is a moral force external to them—society. In every society, there are certain ideas of relative values, rewards, and comfort appropriate to each position—a type of standard that defines the goals to which each strata may legitimately aspire. These define the limits to fix on, and ends or goals are set to the passions. Limitation makes us content with our lot in life, and the individual loves what they have and does not fix their desires on what they lack. Individuals must be satisfied with their lot in life.

Without limits, appetites keep increasing, remaining unquenched, causing constant cravings and continual dissatisfaction that soon become intolerably frustrating, which is ended with destructive anger. Therefore, while society must create these appetites, it must, at the same time, also limit those appetites lest individual's desires grow unchecked creating widespread dissatisfaction.

Society creates these appetites in individuals to motivate them to perform the necessary tasks to sustain collective life. The desire for children is inculcated in individuals in order to replace the depleted population loss through death so society can persist. The desire to work and earn money motivates individuals to accomplish the necessary tasks to maintain society and collective life.

He further states society, and its moral system, is not only something attracting the sentiments and activities of individuals with unequal force but also should be attracting the population as a whole by creating a moral center that produces order and predictability in society, while remaining the central power controlling them.

Durkheim postulates a relationship between the severity of regulation of individual's appetites and the suicide rate in the same fashion as he postulated one between integration and the suicide rates earlier. He labeled this second force regulation referring to the way society regulated appetites in relation to the opportunities available to fulfill those appetites.

A key idea in Durkheim's theory of anomie is that for society to function properly, individuals must have the feeling that a sufficient number of their appetites will be satisfied to be motivated to continue their social existence. In order for this to happen, society must limit individuals' appetites to what is possible in their circumstance lest these become insatiable producing increasing dissatisfaction among members of society.

Durkheim's theory explains how regulation attaches us to society. Regulation attaches individuals to society by creating and meeting a sufficient number of socially generated appetites or desires to make individuals satisfied with their social existences. Society failing to limit an individual's aspirations will create dissatisfaction within an individual's social existence. This failure to attach them to society frees an individual to take their life or harm society. It goes without saying their biological requirements must also be met for society to persist.

The lack of restraints on appetites disrupts the needed balance between ends and means that attaches individuals to society. The breaking of these social bonds then leads to individual and collective acts of self-annihilation through this condition of normlessness. The fading of this sector of norms that regulate appetites unleashes a more angry and violent response of self-annihilation and even of annihilation of society than the disintegration Durkheim describes in the case of integration where individuals experience melancholy rather than anger.

A second cause of anomie: Durkheim identified a second cause of anomie, in addition to cultural values that created unquenchable appetites, in three other conditions in modern society. The three conditions were economic fluctuations, crises, and periods of rapid social change. All these conditions point to the failure of norms to constrain appetites. He did not, however, explicate all the steps by which the three conditions created anomie. An effort will be made to tease out the ways in which these situations cause problems regulating the social appetites of individuals in them and subsequently create anomie, as Durkheim viewed anomie as a consequence of regulation gone awry.

The first cause of anomie Durkheim identified was goals or appetites that explicitly excluded limits like the acquisition of wealth, where the sky is the limit and an all-consuming greed the consequence. This highlights the critical importance of constraining appetites to prevent anomie. The next step teasing out how these conditions cause anomie is identifying *what goes wrong in the three conditions that impair society's ability to regulate individuals' appetites? Because Durkheim had no empirical measures of the degree of anomie, he could not specify what degree of constraint is necessary for society to function optimally and avoid anomie.* A clue may be found in Durkheim's theory of how regulation attaches individuals to society. It does so by permitting individuals enough satisfaction in achieving their goals to make their life worthwhile enough to continue living. To achieve this end, society must create a balance between individuals' goals and the opportunities to obtain them. Durkheim also does not specify what degree of gratification of the population's desires is necessary for optimal societal functioning nor does he indicate the relative importance of restraints versus the existence of opportunities, because if the goals are not available in society, then the degree of restraint is irrelevant.

However, the case Durkheim made for the existence of regulation and his theory of anomie was much less elaborate than the one he made for integration and his theory of egoistic suicide. It was also less supported by facts, comparisons of suicide rates, and had no tests of his hypothesis. This has led to divergent interpretations of his overall theory and critiques that the two forces were indistinguishable (Johnson 1965; Gibbs and Martin 1956, 1964). Also, he did not support his claim of elevated suicide rates in the two of the three contexts he cited, and he only briefly examined how one condition led to a breakdown in regulation.

Let us examine how these three social conditions weaken restraints and produce anomie though there are many gaps in Durkheim's formulations:

Economic fluctuations: Durkheim asserted economic downturns increased suicides but not because they increased poverty. Poverty is a protection against suicide; both poor countries and poor individuals within countries have low suicide rates. The significant factor about economic downturns and all economic fluctuations is that they are moral crises—*disturbances of the moral order.*

Economic fluctuations result in declassification, alter the social hierarchy, and threaten individual's expectations of the social rewards to which they are entitled by virtue of their position in society.

These disruptions of the moral system result in increased suicides, because they disturb *the equilibrium society must maintain between individual's expectations of a certain standard of living and goals to which they should aspire and what is possible to attain in their circumstances.* The failure of society to balance appetites with opportunities leads to frustration and anger and fails to bond individuals sufficiently to society, resulting in their susceptibility to these social forces and high rates of suicide.

Economic upturns should be equally unsettling and increase suicide rates. Poverty protects us because it is a restraint upon our aspirations. Economic upturns can stimulate desires beyond society's capability of satisfying them and cause anomie, like the first cause of anomie Durkheim examined. Or, it may also operate as a moral crisis upsetting existing standards and expectations.

"Sudden Wealth Syndrome" is used to describe the plight of some Silicon Valley millionaires and lottery winners by psychotherapists. The unsettling nature of the experience supports Durkheim's interpretation of the effect of abrupt change, even though positive. It causes personal disequilibrium and suffering. However, there are no reports of suicide to support increased suicides among dot-com billionaires or lottery winners or among the general population during economic upturns.

Durkheim also asserts the two social forces, integration and regulation, influence the system of beliefs and knowledge society creates that also contribute to suicide. When regulation is excessive and societies do not regulate aspirations, it will give rise to the belief that "man is eternally dissatisfied." In the same way, the lack of integration gives rise to beliefs that "life is empty and devoid of meaning." Both beliefs create understandings sympathetic to suicide, reflecting the forces' impact on society. These sentiments are personalizations of the two social forces. They also illustrate aspects of Durkheim's theory of the sociology of knowledge.

Crises also produce anomic conditions though Durkheim does little by way of elaboration of the process of how crises produce suicide. He assumes they alter the understood relationship between "means and ends" and "effort and attainment." Yet not all crises have this effect, he cites war uniting society, increasing integration, and lowering suicide rates earlier in the text in his analysis of integration. It is clear greater specification of the nature of crises is needed to make predictions about the rise of anomie.

Periods of rapid social change also impair the working standards and guidelines that regulate social life and the balance between means and ends in society. This is an especially disruptive factor in modern society as the pace of change is accelerating creating what some have described as "future shock" (Toffler 1984), creating anomie more and more in modern times. Durkheim also did not give examples of how this condition specifically produces anomie or support his claims with statistical comparisons.

The three conditions Durkheim identified creating anomie appeared to cause disequilibrium in the norms balancing means and ends. This resulted from changes in society that made the norms inapplicable to the new conditions thus impairing the norm's ability to restrain individuals' appetites.

This resulted in personal disequilibrium whereby individual's desires are not attuned to the possibilities of attaining the goals causing acute suffering. This anomie is caused by a failure of society to morally restrain individual's desires and to keep the balance between means and ends in those conditions in society. In all three of these conditions, it is the absence of functioning norms that fails to restrain desires and regulate the balance between means and ends and bond individuals to society that causes anomie. This failure makes individuals easy prey to be swept up by their frustration and anger in self-destructive actions causing high suicide rates.

In these conditions, anomie appears to be temporary until new norms emerge to redefine the standards applicable to the new conditions. Until readjustments take place in the social order, individuals are cast adrift without guidelines with respect to where they are and their prospects of achieving their goals. The normal social regulation of the individual's aspirations is disrupted and subsequently has grave consequences for the individual.

What appears common to the three conditions, economic fluctuations, crises, and periods of rapid social change, is that changing social conditions rendered the previous standards inapplicable to the current conditions and new guidelines had not yet emerged. Thus, the lack of operative guidelines emerged in the three conditions as a result of social change which could not restrain appetites resulting in devastating consequences and high rates of suicide, though Durkheim did not produce data in two of the conditions to support those claims. Thus, anomie did not occur in the same fashion prosperous and capitalistic societies produced it, by creating individuals with unquenchable desires. Instead, they created anomie by the absence of norms or guidelines restraining individual's desires. The precipitating factor was social change, and presumably the anomie was only temporary as social guidelines would normally evolve in time. The relations between economic fluctuations and suicide rates also alerted Durkheim to the existence of the second social force, regulation, to explain those facts seemingly not accountable for by integration.

To this point, Durkheim states that appetites must be limited in a given society for it to be properly regulated; however, to be more precise, appetites must be regulated in proportion to the given opportunities within a society. The goals set in one society may not be transferable to another society if their available opportunities are not equal.

In the first two causes, it is the absence of the regulation of appetites that causes anomie. The third cause, perhaps more attributed to Durkheim than actually found in *Suicide*, views social structures that limit access to goals for certain sectors of the population creating the imbalance between ends and means and not the regulation processes.

A third cause of anomie is attributed to Durkheim by Merton in his classic article "Social Structure and Anomie" (1968). Merton argues that anomie primarily results from the social structure or organization of society acting as a barrier limiting access to certain sectors of the society from attaining their goals. Merton's emphasis shifted from the moral restraints regulating people's desires to the opportunities realistically available to them leading to similar frustrations. Merton's interpretation of anomie is the most commonly cited source though its roots are hard to trace in *Suicide* (1897). Merton's conception of anomie appears rooted in Durkheim's analysis of anomic divisions of labor and not in his theory of integration and social order as found in *Suicide* (1897). This will be examined in more depth later.

The suicides discussed in this section were for Durkheim a function of the lack of sufficient constraint on people's appetites. Just as insufficient regulation can cause suicide, Durkheim argues excessive regulation also causes a fourth type of suicide, fatalistic suicide.

The fourth type of suicide: Fatalistic

Just as under-regulation leads to anomic suicide, Durkheim argues the theoretical possibility that over-regulation can have the same effect and labels these as fatalistic suicides. However, it is notable that he only relegated fatalistic suicide to a footnote and a few paragraphs rather than a full chapter. Perhaps it is little discussed due to it being either an afterthought, such a rarity in modern society that it warrants little scrutiny or raised too great a challenge for the symmetry of his theory.[7] Therefore, much of the discussion here is speculative since Durkheim does not describe in depth the process and cause of this type of condition.

Durkheim asserts fatalistic suicide results from rules that are over-confining which also cause goals to be unreachable. It is suicide resulting from *excessive regulation*. The plight of slaves in the past or prisoners in current times might reflect such circumstances. Pointedly, Durkheim gives no examples of overly restrictive norms. Durkheim did not give many examples of fatalistic suicide that fit with his theory illustrating that norms impaired the satisfaction of appetites. Early Christianity that emphasized asceticism and poverty may reflect such norms. A question that arises is: does asceticism interfere with receiving sufficient gratifications to bond individuals to society?

The examples that Durkheim provides are more related to aspects of the social structure limiting opportunities rather than the norms themselves preventing people from achieving their goals.

In fatalistic suicide, it is the over-regulation of behavior and lack of opportunity to attain goals due to the overall organization of society where it may provide no avenues or creates structural barriers that impede goal attainment or where the society is incapable of providing satisfactions of appetites. Durkheim does not explicitly outline this; however, these conclusions can be drawn from the examples Durkheim lists following his definition of fatalistic suicide and provides contemporary relevance for fatalistic suicide. Regardless of how the means are restricted, the goals are not attainable for the individuals in question, which makes life not worthwhile.

Regulation, like integration, attaches individuals to social life and society. In contrast to integration, it does so by creating social appetites that can be realistically satisfied at a level which motivates individuals to continue living in the contexts and circumstances in which they find themselves. Failure to receive sufficient satisfaction from participating in society weakens their desires to live and their ties to life.

Society failing to regulate appetites leads to an infinity of desires and continual frustration with life as does too strongly restraining the satisfaction of desires also makes life unsatisfying, and both conditions lead to suicide.

Durkheim emphasizes excessive regulation of appetites whereas Merton stresses the social structure barring or limiting opportunities. Merton's analysis of anomic suicide seems to have more in common with Durkheim's analysis of fatalistic suicide, since the problems result from the way society is organized and what is possible for individuals to attain by virtue of their position in society. Durkheim's notion of fatalistic suicide results from norms that limit almost all opportunities for a class of individuals or all individuals in society. Merton's theory describes a social structure which limits opportunities for segments of society. The social structure for Merton causes the imbalance between means and ends. This is equivalent to the degree of imbalance between the appetites and opportunities in "Durkheim's terms."

Both Durkheim and Merton do not discuss the origins of such extreme inequality in society. Neither Durkheim nor Merton acknowledges that powerful groups can shape the character of society and transform modern democracies into rigid totalitarian societies with extreme inequality. Contemporary society is manifesting a condition where most of the opportunities to obtain social rewards are in the hands of corporate oligarchs and plutocrats which may reflect worldwide regression toward feudalism. Yet, we can see in the U.S. today that the power these groups exert over government has achieved such control that they have hollowed out what was the middle class and almost impoverished the working and lower classes to the point of historic inequality. This concentration of power in the wealthiest prevents the majority of society from attaining security and upward mobility.

Durkheim's discussion of fatalistic suicide referred to a kind of society that had many similar characteristics to the one described above. It is not clear the specific societies that Durkheim is referring to whether they be nobility and serfdom or masters and slaves, but I am describing societies where the masses have "futures pitilessly blocked and passions violently choked by" structures of power and wealth (1952:239).

Suicides as acts of social protests were not specifically discussed by Durkheim but are related to fatalistic suicide when all avenues are perceived as blocked in accomplishing people's objectives. Farmers in India whose farms cannot provide a living, recent Foxconn factory workers in China, Buddhist priests who set themselves on fire protesting war, and hunger strikes in prisons can reflect fatalistic or altruistic components depending on how the acts of self-destruction are constructed. Revenge suicides are directed toward the external effects that are intended. An example would be seemingly senseless mass shootings that result in self and societal annihilation for those with a hopeless future. Death in protests, however, may not be their intention, but an undesired byproduct of a bargaining strategy and therefore would not be suicide. Many deaths of despair recently have a strong relationship to suicide although it may seem the intentionality of the act is more obscure, but the effects in death are as predictable as suicide.

Though Merton's theory is associated with anomic suicide, a deeper examination shows that it may have more in common with fatalistic suicide, because it identifies the social structure and society as the impediment to satisfying appetites in the same way Durkheim viewed overly restrictive norms impairing the satisfaction of appetites. Whereas Durkheim's identification of the causes of anomie pointed to the failure of restraints, his explanation of fatalistic suicide pointed to the structural obstacles impairing goal attainment. Merton's contribution is to see Durkheim's analysis of fatalistic suicide in contemporary terms whereby aspects of the social structure impair access to goals, which is evidenced by modern society's decimation of the working and middle classes that limit upward mobility. In conclusion, the central difference in Durkheim and Merton's contributions to understanding fatalistic suicide is that Durkheim focuses on the norms impairing individual's abilities to accomplish their goals and that Merton focuses on the structural barriers of society limiting goal attainment, which Durkheim also employs but does not acknowledge. This allows for a more contemporary analysis of the historical hierarchical organization of society.

Comparison of anomic and fatalistic suicides

Anomic and fatalistic suicide both result from under-regulation and over-regulation, respectively. To an individual, these conditions result in a similar feeling of being unable to reach a goal; however, the manner in which this state is reached differs. The first two causes of anomic suicide result from unsatisfiable goals or society's failure to limit aspirations, both causing frustrations that ultimately contribute to suicide. The third cause of anomie was the structural barriers that limited access to these goals. All three conditions created unbearable frustration that found its outlet in self and social annihilation. The resulting frustration and anger from unachievable goals can result in not only a destruction of an individual's life but also in a redirection of the anger to what is perceived as the barrier to the goals, resulting in social annihilation like mass and school shootings. Fatalism also limited many individual's access to goals by the ways society was organized. This created even more widespread frustration and suicide. Anomic suicide results from the unrealistic setting of goals and reality creates the barriers to attaining them. Fatalistic suicide results from the realistic setting of goals and the unfair limitations of the individual throughout society preventing the attaining of them.

Merton assumed his theory articulated Durkheim's theory of anomie, but it did not. In Durkheim's theory, the two causes of anomie were limitless desires and social change that diminished the norms ability to restrain appetites. In Merton's analysis, the failure to satisfy appetites was caused by the organization of societies, that is, the social structure impaired goal attainment. This is more related to Durkheim's analysis of how fatalistic suicide resulted. Goal disjunction refers to patterns of interaction or social structures that impeded people's opportunity to satisfy their appetites; however, Merton limited the obstructions to selected groups rather than to the wider segments of society. By expanding Merton's conception of goal disjunction and applying it to society as a whole, a modern conception of fatalism can be understood, where people's ability to attain their goals is not limited by specific barriers but by widespread inaccessibility to goals via economic barriers through the hierarchical organization of society very much like earlier oppressive and restrictive social structures.

Comparison of the four types of suicide

All four types of suicide, egoistic, altruistic, anomic, and fatalistic, can be viewed as a function of how strongly society attaches individuals to it. Attachment to society through integration occurs as a result of the moral system's extensive control over individual's behavior. Egoistic and altruistic suicides result from insufficient or excessive degrees of integration. Insufficient and extreme attachment work in different ways to cause suicide involving different causal linkages. The strength of the social forces causing suicide is dependent on the ways individuals are *integrated into society* and gives rise to the volume and types of suicide.

Individuals are integrated into the social order through a widely shared powerful normative system that controls extended areas of their lives adhering them to society by extensive social control. In insufficiently integrated societies, egoistic suicides predominate resulting from society's lack of sufficient control over their behavior. The lack of sufficient integration causes suicide in several different ways:

1 It gives rise to sentiments like meaninglessness or purposelessness that impel individuals toward suicide.

2 It can intensify already existing suicidal impulses from other sources like the lack of social connections.
3 It fails to restrain suicidal impulses from any source as individuals assume the right to dispose of themselves.

In highly integrated societies, individuals relinquish the power to take their life and only do so when society demands or permits it, whereas in weakly integrated societies individuals assume the right to make that decision in the face of societal expectations.

Anomic and fatalistic suicides also can be viewed as a result of a failure of regulation to attach individuals sufficiently to society. Regulation attaches people to society differently than integration. Whereas integration attaches people to society through shared norms and values, regulation attaches people by creating and satisfying their appetites in balance with the opportunities that are available, thus, making life worthwhile. Inadequate or excessive regulation leads to increased anomic and fatalistic suicide, respectively.

Both conditions of anomie and fatalism lead to individuals being frustrated in their efforts to obtain sufficient rewards to make life worthwhile. The lack of regulation of social appetites makes them limitless creating an infinity of desires leading to unbearable frustration making life not worthwhile and subsequently suicide. Unless desires are restrained by society, individuals cannot feel content with their lot in life. Over-regulation, where society thwarts every avenue for satisfying one's appetites, similarly leads to frustration and a state where life is insufficiently satisfying to continue living.

Different mechanisms are involved in how integration and regulation attach individuals to society and are produced by different social conditions. Integration attaches individuals by a shared extensive and powerful system of norms that regulates behavior. Regulation attaches individuals by society satisfactorily proportioning individual's aspirations to what is realistically achievable in their social circumstances. Satisfactorily fulfilling their social appetites attaches them to society rather than controlling their behavior as in the case of integration. That is accomplished by society adequately regulating their desires proportionately to their means so as to make the satisfactions they receive from living sufficiently rewarding to motivate them to continue living. What adheres them to society is the experience and expectation of receiving sufficient gratification to make life worth living. Too little or too much regulation in relation to the opportunities available makes life frustrating and unbearable.

In egoism, it is about whether society has sufficient control over individual's lives, and with respect to regulation, it is about whether society moderates their appetites and desires, so they are content enough to continue living with the rewards available in their circumstances. Durkheim assumes individuals make decisions about living based on the relation of their expectations to the satisfactions they receive from life.

In egoistic suicide, people no longer find a basis for existence in life, while in altruistic suicide the basis for existence appears to be situated beyond life itself. In anomic and fatalistic suicide, the basis for existence is feeling sufficiently satisfied with what society provides after it has modulated their desires.

Three of the four types of suicide, egoistic, anomic and fatalistic, result from insufficient attachment to society, and the fourth, altruistic suicide, results from the over-attachment to a society that requires self-sacrifice. Some altruistic suicides could be viewed as resulting from the group severing the attachment when individuals face disgrace, failure, rejection or shame. Other forms of altruistic suicide affirm bonds with the group by conforming to group expectations, as in obligatory, optional, or prestige, where the individual demonstrates their attachment to society through the act of suicide.

Anomic and egoistic suicide both result from society's insufficient presence in the individual. In egoistic states, it is deficient in collective activity depriving the person of meaning and purpose. In anomic states, its influence is lacking in the basic passions where there are not sufficient checks on them. Fatalistic and altruistic suicide result from the extreme presence of society in the individual.

Integration and regulation are, in principle, independent of each other. *All four types of suicide are related to the character and organization of norms in society*, specifically in the degree to which the normative system: (a) integrates groups by virtue of shared beliefs and practices, and (b) regulates member's aspirations in proportion to the opportunities available. Where the norms rigorously guide the individual, egoistic suicide is low. Altruistic suicide occurs in tightly knit societies if the norms require or encourage it or if members fail to live up to group expectations and anticipate exclusion. Where norms regulate desires proportional to available opportunities, anomic and fatalistic suicide rates will be low.

How individuals are integrated and regulated by the normative structure is the critical factor in determining each of the four types of suicide:

1 If groups lack adequate integration then high rates of egoistic suicide will occur.
2 If groups are over-integrated and norms require or encourage suicide, then high rates of altruistic suicide will occur.
3 If group norms do not regulate appetites, then high rates of anomic suicide will occur.
4 If groups regulate aspirations but highly restrict avenues for fulfilling goals, then high rates of fatalistic suicide will occur.

The strength of each force will determine the volume of each type of suicide, and changes in their strength will be reflected in changes in the suicide rate.

Relation between integration and regulation

Durkheim does not elaborate on the relationships between integration and regulation other than both forces decline in modern society and are responsible for increases in the suicide rate. As these forces weaken, increases in both egoistic and anomic suicides are responsible for the rise in suicides in modern society. Altruistic and fatalistic suicides are caused by highly integrated and excessively regulated pre-modern societies but can be found in pockets of modern societies in highly integrated groups like the military and overly regulated ones like prisons.

Some scholars, however, have argued the two forces, integration and regulation, are indistinguishable and can be reduced to a singular force (Johnson 1965; Gibbs and Martin 1956, 1964) as both refer to control over the individual's behavior by society. They argue integration and regulation should be viewed as inseparable ends of a single continuum where high and low levels represent strong and weak societal control over individuals' behavior.

Durkheim might respond that integration refers to societal control over behavior, and conformity and shared awareness is its hallmark. Regulation refers to society's ability to balance individual's appetites or aspirations with sufficient opportunities to sustain their lives. Society has to restrain an individual's wants in proportion to its ability to satisfy a sufficient number of their desires (Muntaner 1996).

Along a similar vein, a related critique is even if the forces were distinguishable, the singling out of the regulation of social appetites, as a distinctive social force, is arbitrary, as there are other factors which if society doesn't regulate, may cause suicides. Society regulates many aspects of individual's behavior that also may be related to suicide, like emotions, so why only single out regulation of social appetites from the others? Emotions, for example, are implicated in suicidal behavior as many suicides have an emotional component, which if not appropriately regulated would also cause suicides. Durkheim noted each force leaves an emotional stamp on individual suicides. For the theory to be complete, all relevant aspects of societal control related to suicide should be identified, or some justification for their exclusion should be made.

It is clear however that the total structure of Durkheim's theory depends on the two forces he identified. Durkheim supports the assertion that there are two distinct forces causing suicide by pointing out regularities in suicide rates caused by each force. A second justification, he offers, is that each force, egoism, altruism, anomie, and fatalism produces a distinctive emotional stamp on the individual's act of suicide, though some individual's response may be a consequence of a blend of forces.

Durkheim postulated the existence of the social force he labeled integration to account for the differences in suicide rates between various religious groups, marital statuses, and states of the polity. He even tested his hypothesis examining variations in degrees of centralization of authority and minority status in the country among religious groups which supported his hypothesis with regard to the degree of integration and suicide rate.

He identified other regularities in the suicide rates that he concluded could not be explained by integration and postulated the existence of a second force, regulation, to account for those regularities. These regularities were: suicide rates increase in economic downturns, crises, and during periods of rapid social change. What these situations have in common, according to Durkheim, is that they are moral crises.

Economic downturns, for example, increase suicide because they are moral crises and not because they increase poverty, because poverty is a protection against suicide. Both poor countries and poor individuals within those countries have low rates of suicide. Economic declines increase suicide because they result in declassification and the loss of guidelines, especially those related to social rankings and progress in individuals reaching their goals that they would have a right to expect in their social positions. The breakdown in or lack of norms during economic fluctuations, crises, and periods of rapid change create disorientation, frustration, and anger that result in self-destructive acts like suicide.

However, when Durkheim discussed the crisis of war earlier in the treatise, he did not view it as a moral crisis increasing suicide but as an event that unified society increasing its integration and decreasing suicides. A possible contradiction in Durkheim's work that lends support to Johnson (1965) and Gibbs and Martin's (1958, 1964) critique that the forces are indistinguishable is Durkheim's defining the absence or lack of norms as a lack of integration and later in his discussion of anomie as a lack of regulation. This inconsistency may be due to Durkheim's incomplete specification and differentiation of the two dimensions, or it may be an actual contradiction in the theory. A last troublesome fact is that economic upturns must also be moral crises, but they don't increase the suicide rate. All of these points need to be addressed.

Further support for Durkheim's claim of two distinctive forces driving suicide in society can be found in his examination of the relations between social causes and individual suicides. He argued that each of the forces had a distinctive impact on individuals' emotional reactions associated with their suicides. The lack of integration and lack of regulation each leave a distinctive stamp on individual suicides.

Individuals exposed to a lack of integration possessed feelings of emptiness, meaninglessness and purposelessness as precursors to their suicides. Whereas individuals exposed to a lack of regulation or anomie suffer stronger reactions like confusion, frustration, or anger similar to those exposed to economic downturns, crises, or periods of rapid change. However, Durkheim had no data to support his claim only illustrations and anecdotal examples. This supports there were two distinct forces that produced different effects on individuals, but he did not present sufficient evidence or clarity to completely dismiss other's critiques that Durkheim did not see deeply enough into the flaws in his conceptual distinctions between the forces.

Better clarification of the differences between integration and regulation, the social conditions that give rise to them, and specification of the intervening variables by which they cause suicides would have avoided problems interpreting Durkheim's theory. If Durkheim specified what is common to economic fluctuations, crises, and periods of rapid social change that make them moral crises and failures of regulation, then this specification would have clarified how they are different from the lack of shared norms weakening integration. This differentiation might have clarified the differences in the nature of the two forces and the role of norms in generating suicide. Are the three situations he describes as moral crises causing anomie ones where the changes upset the balance between the means and desired ends? Whereas stable conditions permit more focus on cohesion and the role of norms in generating mechanical solidarity and strong societal control. Materialism and capitalism create similar imbalances between means and ends by failing to limit appetites thus also creating anomie. Other social conditions like the rise of social structural barriers or patterns of discrimination, extreme inequality, or crypto capitalism that shrink opportunities cause similar imbalances in society and anomie but are not discussed by Durkheim. He also did not address why economic upturns, which were also moral crises, do not increase suicide. Henry and Short (1954) offer a more nuanced analysis of the relation between economic fluctuations and suicide rates noting their differential impacts on various classes and differences in responses to the economic disruptions.

Another factor contributing to the diverse interpretations of Durkheim's theory is that norms play different roles in integration and regulation, producing the different types of suicides. In integration, shared norms produce strong centripetal forces, which Durkheim labeled mechanical solidarity, that form strong bonds uniting individuals and adhering members to the group. Few shared norms in a group create weak bonds and high rates of egoistic suicides. Mechanical solidarity is the fundamental social glue holding all societies together.

A second way norms bond individuals to groups creating integration is through their power to control conduct and the extensiveness of social life they cover. Powerful norms manifest high levels of conformity and if they cover extensive areas of life, society has a tight grip on their members and, consequently, few abandon their obligation to society through suicide. Integration, through a system of powerful and extensive norms creates a system of strong societal control and tight bonds to society and low rates of egoistic suicides.

Durkheim does not explicitly make this distinction and highlights shared norms as integration at one point and strong and pervasive norms at another point as though they are both components of integration or they are both part of the definition of integration or both contribute to integration which makes his theory less clear. Both shared norms and powerful norms unify and integrate society, preventing suicides by tightly bonding individuals to society making them part of a larger whole. The lack of integration is both a necessary and sufficient condition to produce high rates of egoistic suicides. The lack of a sufficient number of shared norms or powerful norms cause egoistic suicide due to the lack of sufficient cohesion in society or a group. Both shared norms and powerful norms act to bond individuals to the group.

The third way norms produce suicide is in highly integrated societies or groups where the norms demand or encourage suicide, and high rates of altruistic suicide will result. It is the content of the norms, not their shared or powerful nature, however, that produces altruistic suicides. The degree of integration only increases the likelihood individuals will conform to the norm and make that sacrifice for the group.

The first two ways norms influence suicide is through their ability to unify and bond individuals to each other and society. The failure of the norms to bond individuals results in egoistic suicide. The third way they produce altruistic suicide in highly integrated societies is through their content. When norms require or encourage individual sacrifice and they are tightly bonded to society group expectations are given more salience than personal desires. Here, integration is a necessary but not sufficient condition to produce suicide. Norms demanding self-sacrifice are also a necessary condition for altruistic suicide.

A fifth way norms produce suicide is when they fail to regulate individual's appetites in proportion to what is attainable in society making life worth living thereby sufficiently attaching them to society. Lack of sufficient regulation by the norms leads to anomic and excessive regulation to fatalistic suicide. Thus, if by insufficient or excessive regulation, the norms fail to attach individuals to society high rates of anomic and fatalistic suicide will result.

If society fails to limit individual's appetites or excessively obstructs opportunities to fulfill them to the point where life is not worthwhile, then both types of suicide will occur. The bonds will not be strong enough to attach them adequately to society if they lack sufficient gratification of their social appetites. A certain level of satisfaction to individuals' social appetites must be gratified to bond them to society otherwise their frustration expresses itself in anomic and fatalistic suicide.

A sixth way norms can produce suicide is their absence during economic fluctuations, rapid social change, and crises Durkheim describes as anomie. The absence of guidelines during change cause disorientation and declassification. Thus, not only does the absence of norms lead to a lack of cohesion through integration but it also causes anomie resulting in disorientation, declassification, and anomic suicides. The norms operate differently in different social contexts to produce the various types of suicide.

Durkheim's failure to elaborate these points also contributes to the divergences in interpreting the theory.

Additionally, he doesn't elaborate aspects of anomic and fatalistic suicide and the role of norms and the role of social structure in limiting opportunities and creating anomie. More clarification of the nature of the forces of integration and regulation, what gives rise to them, and how they cause suicide is central to understanding Durkheim's theory.

Durkheim's distinction between the forces of integration and regulation showed he clearly regarded society's control over behavior separately from its regulation of aspirations which he supported by their different effects on regularities in suicide rates and emotions related to the type of suicides they generated. The regulation of emotion perhaps should also be considered since Durkheim believed feelings were also capable of creating bonds in small families, and that suicide is sometimes a passionate act where emotions rule. More clarity is needed in whether regulation diminishes with integration, or if it is independent of integration. Regulation is restricted to its ability to restrain appetites to what is realistically attainable, and they are balanced enough to sufficiently motivate individuals to continue living. Regulation needs further elaboration, especially whether aspects outside the moral structure can restrain them like the experience of poverty or the role of the social structure and social context.

Monogamy, for example, is an institution comprised of moral expectations that limits the number of spouses that are acceptable, so appetites do not keep expanding unchecked. Yet monogamy can have different effects in different social contexts. When people marry in the U.S. today, they stop sleeping with others and may experience this as a restraint or deprivation to which many respond with extra-marital affairs. But monogamy may be experienced differently in societies which restrict sex prior to marriage, so that marriage offers satisfactions previously denied while checking desires for more mates. In both cases, monogamy restricts the number of spouses but produces different levels of dissatisfaction. Furthermore, devastating wars may reduce the number of males for women to marry, creating barriers unrelated to moral regulation.

Durkheim also believed modern consumer capitalism encouraged materialism and insatiable greed as well as frequent economic crises which cause extreme deregulation leading to frustration and suicide. The emphasis on accumulation of wealth made individuals feel less pervious to societal restraint and thus anomie.

Another example of deregulation caused solely by the moral structure are cultural conflicts where social values conflict with each other. For example, the emphasis on "winning" conflicts with the value of "being liked" in a bureaucratic society where "nice guys finish last." These examples illustrate problems in regulation occurring primarily within the moral structure of society. Some have reinterpreted Durkheim's theory that anomie is a result of conflict between cultural goals and barriers created by the social structure labeled goal disjunction and called strain theory (Merton 1968).

Whereas Durkheim identified the cause of anomie as a failure of the moral system to adequately restrain social appetites creating limitless appetites and perpetual frustration, Merton identified the disjunction caused by the social structure impairing opportunities for certain segments of the population. When the social structure acts as a barrier to individuals attaining their goals, pressures build to violate the norms creating a state of normlessness and a state of anomie.

Despite Merton's interpretation departing substantially from Durkheim's theory of anomie, it has become the most cited source. Merton asserts the cause of anomie is the existence of social structural barriers that limit opportunities to attain cultural goals for certain sectors of the population. The frustration of individuals facing blocked opportunities provides the motivation to delegitimate the norms creating anomie. Whereas Durkheim asserts the primary cause of anomie is the failure of society's moral system to establish satiation points that limit individual's appetites to prevent insatiable desires and anomie, not blocked opportunities. Durkheim identified other conditions that the lack of norms also upset the balance between appetites and opportunities such as economic fluctuations, crises, and rapid social change that cause anomie.

Merton asserts the cause of anomie is in the social structure's limiting access to goals while Durkheim asserts it is the lack of a regulatory mechanism in the moral system to limit individual's social appetites. For Merton, the problem giving rise to anomie is in the social structure, and for Durkheim, it is in the moral system of norms and values. In capitalist societies like the U.S., studies show that no matter how much wealth individuals have; they would like twenty percent more. Merton's analysis of anomie seems more related to fatalistic suicide where society makes it impossible for people to attain their goals rather than Durkheim's analysis of anomic suicide and pursuing limitless or impossible goals and the inevitable frustration that brings.

To eliminate anomie according to Merton's analysis, society would provide sufficient opportunities for individuals to achieve what people in their social position have a right to expect. Whereas Durkheim's analysis suggests a change in the culture and moral system de-emphasizing materialism and self-interest and imposing norms and values limiting appetites to eliminate anomie.

Because Merton focuses on all forms of non-conformity or deviance, he sees anomic pressures greatest on those at the bottom of social hierarchies as his focus is on norms limiting conduct. Whereas Durkheim limits his analysis of anomie to acts of self-destruction or suicide more likely in the upper strata of society and on the norms regulating appetites not conduct. Durkheim suggests other social conditions like economic fluctuations, crises, and periods of rapid social change also impair the norm's ability to regulate appetites.

Merton's analysis implies the problem of anomie can be resolved by eliminating the structural barriers, whereas Durkheim believes the moral system of capitalism itself must be transformed to balance self-interest with responsibility to the larger society. In this sense, Durkheim is more radical than Merton's reformist approach in regard to their solution to anomie.

Durkheim's theory does not address the role of the social structure in either creating anomie or in shaping individual responses to anomie, which is central to Merton's theory. Thus, much of the difficulty in interpreting Durkheim's theory is due to ambiguity he created by not elaborating on the differences between integration and regulation and how they each contribute to the various types of suicide.

One reason for the discrepancy between Merton and Durkheim's theory of anomie is that Merton's theory is rooted in *The Division of Labor* in Durkheim's discussion of anomic divisions of labor. Merton's theory is oriented toward the problem of social order and how the organization of society itself creates disorder. Merton's theory is concerned with the conditions under which norms weaken and noncompliance to them increases, creating social disorder. Thus, it is oriented more toward integration rather than regulation, due to Merton's conception of anomie being related to the weakening of norms not the regulation of appetites. On the other hand, Durkheim's discussion of anomie in *Suicide* is focused totally on regulating appetites to achieve a balance between appetites and opportunities, minimizing suicidal behavior by properly attaching individuals to society. This is equivalent to Merton's balancing of ends and means which minimizes all deviant behavior by attaching individuals to each other through shared norms and values. Merton asserts that in order to ensure conformity to norms, some rewards must accrue for mere conformity to the norms, revealing his concern with deviance, not cohesion. According to Durkheim, normlessness with regard to anomie refers to the absence of norms constraining appetites. Whereas, according to Merton, it refers to norms not regulating conduct. Thus, Merton's discussion of anomie is oriented toward integration while Durkheim's discussion is addressed toward regulation in society though these are frequently confounded with each other by scholars.

Notes

1 These facts have been questioned by Pope (1976).
2 Durkheim failed to control for religion or class, both of which are associated with family size and suicide rates.
3 To be discussed later, Scheff's characterization of attunement versus engulfment or strong versus weak levels of social control are relevant as similar ways of describing the individual's relation to society.
4 Foucault (1975) highlighted modern society's increasing efforts to exercise control through surveillance, and recently, Hariri (2015) claims modern technology can surveil the whole population, 24 hours a day, even more thoroughly including internal states of the body and mind with devices that can detect emotions toward leaders in China and the U.S. than small societies could in the past. The question which can be raised to Durkheim is even if it increases social control, does it increase cohesion and solidarity?
5 After the Vietnam War, the military incorporated the importance of strong interpersonal social bonds in unit effectiveness (Shills and Janowitz 1948, Stouffer et al 1949) and withdrew whole units from combat to replace missing soldiers to rebuild unit solidarity before returning them to combat, and in the Iraq and Afghanistan wars, seriously injured soldiers express strong desires to return to combat as their buddies need their help. It should be noted that these *studies support the importance of interpersonal relationships over moral sentiments like patriotism as the important social bond creating unit cohesion and a willingness to sacrifice your life*. Soldiers do not risk their life for patriotism or other moral beliefs but for the sake of primary relationships (Stouffer et al 1949).
6 This reflects the debate between Comte, who viewed society as primarily altruistic, devoted to collective interests, and Spencer, who viewed society as more egoistic, driven by self-interest. Durkheim reconceptualized the debate as a dimension or variable, integration, along which societies could vary, and it was a question of the relative balance of emphasis of any particular society.
7 Supportive of fatalism being an afterthought is the fact that when he identified the currents causing suicide he omitted fatalism (1952:264).

4

MACRO–MICRO RELATIONS AND INDIVIDUAL ACTS OF SUICIDE

Relations between social causes and individual suicides

Both Durkheim's second objective, to show how the social causes produce suicide, and his third objective, to identify the relation of social causes to individual acts of suicide, will be explored in this chapter. In pursuing this second objective in his theory of suicide, he enunciates the intervening variables and causal nexuses between the social forces, integration and regulation, and suicide. Durkheim's third and final objective in *Suicide* was to identify the connections between social causes and individual suicides (1952:li).

Why the lack of integration causes egoistic suicide: the causal nexuses

Durkheim further pursues the second objective of his theory of suicide by identifying the ways social causes produce their effects within the context of egoistic suicide. It also sheds light on his third objective by identifying the relationship of social causes to individual acts of suicide. This aspect of Durkheim's theory explores how insufficient integration causes suicide. However, rather than a singular explanation, Durkheim offers several reasons why the lack of integration causes suicide with each explanation involving different causal linkages relating low integration to suicide. This also permits an investigation of whether these hypotheses can specify individual acts of suicide as well. These explanations proposed by Durkheim have differing levels of development, sophistication, and thought; however, issues arise in comparing these explanations to one another since Durkheim

DOI: 10.4324/9781003669272-4

did not specify or recognize how each mechanism interacts with the others causing contradiction. Some are of primary importance while others only of secondary importance; some of his explanations are straight forward, and others more complex and less well-developed involving factors Durkheim did not specify or recognize how each mechanism interacts with the others. He provided no supporting evidence for each of the explanations he proposes.

The following explanations represent various hypotheses Durkheim sets for why low degrees of integration cause high rates of egoistic suicide.

1. *Individual Feelings of Meaninglessness*: The foremost reason, according to Durkheim, is that low integration (few common beliefs or practices) leads to feelings of meaningless or purposelessness in individuals, which, in turn, cause them to not only to feel life is not worthwhile but to take their lives. If the individual isolates himself, it is because *the ties uniting him with others are slackened* or broken, because society is not sufficiently integrated *at the points they are in contact with.* The gap between one and another individual conscience, estranging them from each other, are authentic results of the weakening of the social forces (1952:281).

Durkheim states that society cannot disintegrate without the individuals detaching themselves from social life. And as they detach themselves from social life, *they lose the very attachments that make life worthwhile.*

He argues that much of the "being" of the civilized person is aroused by society, which fills the individual with religious, political, or moral beliefs that control their actions. These beliefs not only have a collective origin, but their very purpose is to serve collective or societal ends. Individuals have no inborn needs to use language, marry, work, or be moral. But, for society to persist, social sentiments must evolve. These sentiments are then directed toward the purpose of group life. These beliefs are society incarnate—individualized in each of us. We cling to these forms of activity only to the extent we cling to society. As we become detached from society, the very source of social meanings, we become detached from those internalized social aspects of ourselves, which is society internalized. If we are not tied to these social ends, then behavior loses the meaning and purpose for which it evolved. And the purpose toward which moral, religious, and political beliefs are oriented—the collective goals—are lost to us as well. Only a believer firm in his or her faith or an individual strongly bound by family or political ties can feel purpose to this life. Uncommitted to social purpose, life loses all meaning and meaninglessness discourages us from going on and gives us no reason to endure life's misfortunes.

Because we are socialized into a social existence, the fading of it leaves us unable to be satisfied without one, and results in feelings of helplessness and emptiness[1]. In such a state of confusion, the least discouragement may give birth to desperate resolutions. If life is not worth the trouble of being alive, everything becomes a pretext to rid ourselves of it.

2. *Collective Sentiments of Meaninglessness:* Durkheim further asserts that not only do individuals respond to these social conditions, but groups also evolve a collective evaluation of the value of existence "inclining people to sadness or cheerfulness, making them see things in bright or somber lights" (1952:213). In weakly integrated groups, pessimistic or negative evaluations of life may evolve which will be communicated to the parts. "Currents of depression and disillusionment emanating from no particular individual but expressing society's state of disintegration" are formed that reflect the relaxation of societal bonds (1952:172). Belief systems evolve in the group, which attest to the senselessness of life, and new moralities commend suicide or minimal existence.

> As these currents are collective, they have, by virtue of their origin, an authority which they impose upon the individual and they drive [them] more vigorously on the way to which [they are] already inclined by the state of moral distress directly aroused in [them] by the disintegration of society.
>
> *(1952:173)*[2]

Ironically, at the same moment the individual frees themself from the social environment by suicide, they submit to its societal influence.

The bond attaching people to life relaxes because the bond that attaches them to society has slackened. The incidents of private life that seem to be the direct inspiration of suicide and are considered its determining causes are, in reality, only incidental causes. The individual yields to the slightest shock of circumstances, because society's state of disintegration has made them ready prey to suicide. The more social the person is, the more points of support outside of themself become necessary. Yet whether these feelings cause suicide, or whether they merely intensify suicidal feelings that arise from other sources, or whether both components are necessary and sufficient conditions for the individual's taking his or her life is not specified by Durkheim.

Durkheim also discusses *secondary* reasons why the lack of integration can lead to suicide.

3. *Intensification of Misfortunes*: According to this hypothesis, the individual's misfortunes, in which the suicidal impulses are rooted, become more intensely felt under conditions of low integration. Thus, the suicidal impulse is intensified.

This intensification is brought about in several ways. First, when the individual has no purpose outside their own existence, any misfortune that occurs is dramatically intensified because of excessive self-concern—the result of there being little else to life but the individual themselves.

> They, on their part, have no reason to endure life's sufferings patiently. For they cling to life more resolutely when belonging to a group they love, so as not to betray interests they put before their own . . . and the lofty goal they envision prevents their feeling personal troubles so deeply.
>
> *(1952:168)*

Because the individual is fixated on the self, misfortunes are more intensely felt absorbing one's total attention. An individual who undergoes a misfortune and who has little involvement in collective goals will experience more deprivation and torment than a similar individual who has a greater involvement in group life.

Second, personal misfortunes also become intensified when group support is lacking. There is, in short, in a cohesive and animated society, a constant interchange of ideas and feelings from each to all, something like a mutual moral support, which instead of throwing the individual on their own resources, leads them to share in the collective energy and supports their own when exhausted (1952:168). Here, Durkheim refers to the network of interpersonal relationships as "integration" rather than an aspect of the moral structure. Groups act as "shock absorbers." When group support is available for individuals during crises, they are more able to successfully cope with them. If two individuals suffer the same misfortune, it will be experienced less intensely and devastatingly by a person who has group support. Rituals such as funerals provide support and reestablish solidarity among group members. Interaction among participants in funerals reknit the torn social fabric from the loss of a member proclaiming the family goes on despite its loss. Thus, two persons suffering from the same objective misfortune will experience them subjectively differently. When groups are loosely integrated, personal troubles are experienced more intensely because individuals are self-centered and lack the group support, strength, and energies to cope with crises. Studies have shown the supportive nature of primary relationships in a variety of contexts like in the military, prisons, street gangs, bureaucracies, work settings, and neighborhoods, among others.

Misfortunes are varied, loss of loved ones, failure, loneliness, betrayal, sickness, etc. Groups support provides collective energies which help the individual to cope with the situation. It can also make them feel loved or less lonely when a loss of a loved person occurs or valued when they have failed in some aspect of life, thus alleviating some of the distress if not some undesirable consequences of it.

Therefore, low integration can either create the suicidal impulse that is caused by individual misfortunes. Durkheim does not discuss the role society plays in creating misfortunes in egoistic suicide. He thinks of them as given properties of life. The predisposition toward suicide then results from the intensity of the suffering experienced by the individual. If troubles are random, group amplification of them or amelioration of them are not, and therefore, low integrated groups cause more suicide by intensifying the individual's sufferings and not buffering misfortunes. Integration is not a direct precipitator of suicide in these cases, rather suicide is a response to the misfortunes.

In some societies, the river of troubles may be a small trickle and in others a gushing torrent of tragedies and misfortunes. The main factor that determines the volume of suicides, however, may not be the level of tragedies and misfortunes in society, but how securely people are bound together by the moral structure. Some moral structures bind people so securely, no one succumbs to suicidal pressures and others so weakly that it provides little protection against the slings and arrows of outrageous fortune, and most who experience misfortune will succumb to it. The more tightly knit the structure, the fewer persons who will be engulfed by the torrent of troubles and dragged over the abyss to suicide.

4. *Weakened Restraints:*

> As collective force is one of the obstacles best calculated to restrain suicide, its weakening involves a development of suicide. When society is strongly integrated, it holds individuals under its control, considers them at its service and thus forbids them to dispose willfully of themselves. Accordingly it opposes their evading their duties to it through death. But how could society impose its supremacy upon them when they refuse to accept its subordination as legitimate?
>
> *(1952:168)*

Durkheim also sees integration as a restraining force upon the individual's desire to take their own life[3]. Suicide is sometimes described as "taking one's life" with the addendum "from society" implied. The theoretical basis lies in the restraining force of society in the form of its culture and social organization. An important point not explored sufficiently by Durkheim is the different bases upon which the group "controls" the individual's behavior. If he is asserting that the culture of the group with its system of norms and legitimate authority controls the individual's behavior, then integration refers to the shared meanings and their ability to regulate conduct. If, however, he is asserting that the restraint of the individual's behavior comes from the social organization, social structure, or interpersonal relationships of the group, then "integration" refers to the structure of interpersonal relationships. Two different intervening processes are possible, and Durkheim never makes explicit the role of each process. This hypothesis does not concern itself with the origin of the suicidal impulse but merely examines the role of society in restraining suicidal impulses that already exist. Obligations, responsibilities, and the claims of others prevent persons who desire to take their life from doing so.

5. *Isolation and Loneliness:* An explanation attributed to Durkheim (Landecker 1950) is that low integration (weak communicative integration or the lack of intimate relationships) leads to weakened relationships and to feelings of isolation and loneliness that are painful and, in turn, lead to suicide. A similar interpretation is that social individuation, fostered by the division of labor or cultural diversity (i.e., normative and functional integration), results in differences in values, practices, and beliefs, which fragments the sense of community and, in turn, leads to social isolation and loneliness. Both these states in society directly produce suicidal impulses in individuals. However, this argument may be more imputed to Durkheim than found in *Suicide*[4]. Travis (1990) linked isolation to Halbwachs' rather than Durkheim's theory of suicide. Fromm (1969) asserts modern society produces a sense of isolation in humans that is the primary source of anxiety and mental turmoil that may be the consequence of *individuation* from the division of labor making persons different from one another. Fromm argues this induced feeling of separateness or apartness and concomitant loneliness is due to social differentiation. Whereas Riesman (2020) characterizes modern society as a "lonely crowd" while Weber emphasizes the expanding bureaucratic organization of social relationships fosters impersonalization, which creates loneliness. Why loneliness leads to suicide is not explored by Durkheim, but this explanation views low integration producing loneliness and suicidal impulses in individuals. This raises the question of a new dimension, other than whether or not connections exist among members of society, but of *the quality of those connections and degrees of intimacy providing healthier connections.*

Thus, several different explanations are offered by Durkheim for why low integration leads to high rates of suicide: individual feelings of meaningless and purposelessness, collective feelings of meaninglessness and purposelessness, and some secondary reasons are also identified: intensification of people's misfortunes, weakened social restraints, and feelings of isolation and loneliness. Each explanation involves different causal mechanisms connecting integration to suicide. Also, each of the social factors operate in different ways: they can cause suicidal motivations, only intensify already existing suicidal impulses, or restrain individuals from acting upon existing suicidal impulses. Further research is required to determine the relative importance of each factor on the rate of suicide, although Durkheim relegates some factors as secondary. In addition, other definitions of integration and their operation at different levels of abstraction must also be fully explored to determine which explanation best fits the facts of suicide.

Durkheim does not specify in much detail as he had with egoistic suicide the intervening variables and causal nexuses, of the other three types of suicide. With regard to altruistic suicide, he implies that those most heavily integrated into cohesive groups such as the military and those who are officers and have served a long time were more likely to follow the norms requiring self-sacrifice than those less integrated into the group. With respect to anomic suicide, those individuals who are most exposed to economic fluctuations such as those working in the area of finance would be the most likely affected in capitalistic societies, but with regard to rapid periods of social change, he did not specify the intervening variables or causal nexuses although he did point to the frustration resulting from unattainable goals due to the lack of constraint. Lastly, with respect to fatalistic suicide, he made no suggestions with regard to the intervening variables. Therefore, few predictions can be made at the individual level, and he explored none, although he pointed toward sentiments of despair in regard to fatalistic suicide.

Durkheim clearly had an interest in the relationships between macro social levels of analysis and micro level individual reactions, though it is the least developed or explored aspect of his theory. Scholars have largely ignored this aspect of Durkheim's theory believing either social system analyses lack implications for predicting individual suicides or that explaining individual suicides is outside of the sociologist's purview.

Durkheim's theory is a prime example of a social system analysis of behavior ordinarily regarded as a personal act. Even though his theory was primarily designed to explain differences in suicide rates between groups, it may also have consequences for specifying which individuals within the group or society will take their lives. Integrating macro and micro analysis can enhance clarity in the chains of causation by which social causes produce their effects, and also this integration can reveal whether the theory has predictive value at the individual level. Such an analysis raises unanticipated questions about the theory. Does Durkheim's macro theory have consequences for micro behavior? Specifically, does his theory of integration have implications for predicting individual instances of suicide even if he did not intend to explain those aspects of suicide? Or, conversely, must separate explanations be proposed to explain macro and micro phenomena, as Gibbs (1968:8) suggests?

Can Durkheim's macro theory of integration be extended to micro predictions of individual egoistic suicides?

Does Durkheim's theory of integration have implications for predicting individual suicides? Can his law of "inverse relation between integration and suicide" be extended to apply to individual egoistic suicides? Does his hypothesis of an "inverse relationship between degrees of integration and suicide rates" at the group level, imply at the individual level that the least integrated persons are most likely to take their lives[5]? For example, because Catholics have a lower suicide rate than Protestants due to their group's higher level of integration, does that imply that the least integrated Catholics should be the ones who are most likely to commit suicide? The logical implications of Durkheim's theory are not clear on this point.

Whether Durkheim's theory of egoism can predict individual suicides varies depending on which of the several explanations he proposed is examined. The intervening variables and chain of causation involved in that explanation of egoistic suicide create numerous conclusions which may be contradictory to each other. Thus, to answer the question whether Durkheim's theory can predict individual instances of egoistic suicide will depend on which explanation of why low integration causes suicide is examined. This aspect of Durkheim's theory of egoistic suicide needs further elaboration of the hypotheses and the possibility they lead to individual predictions. Durkheim does not explore this question in *Suicide* (1897).

Durkheim's theory of egoistic suicide, as revealed earlier, contains several different hypotheses of the role of integration causing egoistic suicide which involve different intervening variables that cause suicide. The various hypotheses focused on individual sentiments of meaninglessness and purposelessness, collective sentiments of meaninglessness and purposelessness, and intensification of misfortunes and weakened restraint. These intervening variables acted as causal mechanisms that illuminated how low degrees of integration contributed to suicide.

Though Durkheim's theory is described as a singular theory, numerous explanations are contained just within his theory of egoistic suicide. If the various interpretations of Durkheim's theory are included, five different definitions of integration can be identified: shared meanings or culture, interaction and intimate relationships or social structure, a balance of egoistic-altruistic and anomic-fatalistic forces or equilibrium of social system, and attunement or intersubjectivity based on social-psychological processes.[6] In addition, five further conceptions of integration can also be identified: organization of the part to the whole and synchronicity, unity, strength of the social bond or cohesion, balance or equilibrium of forces, and social control which can refer to three different units (persons, group standards, or behavior) at several levels of analysis (society, community, group, relationship, and individuals) that could involve numerous intervening processes or causal nexus between low integration and suicide (individual sentiments and collective representations of meaninglessness, intensification of misfortunes, weakened restraints, and loneliness-isolation). Numerous permutations of just these variables can be generated as possible hypotheses to account for egoistic suicide. Not all permutations, however, are logically consistent, and several interpretations in the literature are not supported by a close reading of Durkheim's work. Nonetheless, several possible explanations are contained within Durkheim's theory of egoistic suicide. Ambiguity is heightened by Durkheim's failure to adequately specify the nature of the intervening variables and the mechanisms by which low integration contributes to suicide rates. The lack of integration can (a) produce suicidal impulses, (b) only intensify already existing suicidal impulses, or (c) merely restrain individuals from acting on already existing suicidal impulses. Thus, in some explanations, integration is a necessary and sufficient condition for suicide, whereas in others, integration only alters the probability of suicide resulting, providing suicidal impulses already exist in a population. Only reasonably plausible permutations within the structure of Durkheim's theory are examined here. Clearly, Durkheim offers several hypotheses as to why the lack of integration results in suicide with each involving different causal links and social processes. We shall also explore whether each explanation has implications for predicting individual suicidal tendencies.

1. *Individual Sentiments of Meaninglessness:* The most plausible interpretation of Durkheim's theory is that the lack of integration refers to a lack of shared moral sentiments. In this sense, the lack of integration leads to weakened social control due to weaker orientation toward social goals, creating sentiments of meaninglessness in individuals, which cause suicidal behavior. The most reasonable interpretation of integration in this instance would be "unity" of the group with respect to social meanings or social regulation. Groups lacking unity produce in individuals' sentiments of purposelessness and meaninglessness that lead to suicidal impulses and acts. Unity is a group attribute—a group characterized by many shared social meanings. At the group level, the hypothesis states that suicide rates would be high in groups that exhibit few shared meanings. Predictions could also be made at the individual level in that sentiments of meaninglessness would be most strongly felt in individuals who were culturally dissimilar, and those would be the most likely to commit suicide. The individual not bound to family, religious, or political norms and beliefs would feel little purpose to life, only emptiness[7]. Here, precipitating events would not be the cause of suicide; anything could trigger the suicidal impulse. The following hypothesis could be proposed:

HYPOTHESIS 1A applies at the group level and can be expressed:

$$SM/TM \times (nIm) = SR$$

SM = shared meanings, TM = total number of meanings, n = number of persons, Im = intensity of suicidal impulses, SR = suicide rate

This hypothesis postulates at the group level of analysis that the proportion of shared meanings in the group will generate a specific number of persons with suicidal impulses sufficient to induce suicidal acts, which, in turn, will lead to a specific suicide rate as long as the proportion specified with the same salience to members. The relationship between increments in shared meanings and increases in suicide rates can then be examined.

HYPOTHESIS 1B applies to the individual level: This interpretation of Durkheim's theory can also generate predictions at the individual level of analysis: those individuals most dissimilar in social meanings will be the ones most likely to commit suicide within the group.

2. *Collective Sentiments of Meaninglessness:* This explanation emphasizes group definitions that incline individuals to feel sadness and hopelessness as a result of collective representations. If shared beliefs can independently produce inclinations toward suicide in the individual, predictions could be made only at the group level and not for specific individuals. Or, if collective sentiments cause suicide, then those individuals most tied to the group's culture would commit suicide, as opposed to Hypothesis 1B focusing on those who were culturally dissimilar. However, it appears that Durkheim gave collective representations only a secondary reinforcing role in his analysis of egoistic suicide.

HYPOTHESIS 2A: $PM/TM > nIm = SR$

PM = pessimistic meanings, TM = total meanings, n = number of persons, Im = intensity of suicidal impulses, SR = suicide rate

This hypothesis postulates at a group level that as the proportion of pessimistic or hopeless meanings increase in a group, the rate of suicide will also increase.

HYPOTHESIS 2B: This hypothesis applies to the individual level and postulates that those *most* integrated would be the most likely to internalize such pessimistic meanings and therefore most likely to commit suicide.

Hypotheses 1 and 2 offer fundamentally different roles for the moral structure's involvement in causing suicide. In Hypothesis 1 it is the absence of the moral structure which creates suicide and in Hypothesis 2 it is the direct impact of moral beliefs that causes suicide[8].

3. *Intensification of Misfortunes:* This approach, which Durkheim regarded as secondary, views the role of society not as creating suicidal impulses, but as amplifying the individual's misfortunes. Suicidal impulses arise from misfortunes and do not necessarily have social origins. "Excessive self-concern,"

a consequence of egoistic societies, increases the intensity of suffering. Cultural diversity (low integration) leads to increased individualism, which heightens self-concern. Because individualism intensifies misfortunes when they arise, it amplifies suicidal impulses in the individual. This interpretation rests upon the notion of integration as shared meanings. Group support reduces the intensity of misfortunes and individual sufferings. Here, Durkheim's referent of "integration" is the network of interpersonal relationships that provide the individual with the support and energy necessary to cope with misfortunes successfully. In both cases, lack of integration does not produce the suicidal impulse; it only intensifies an impulse arising from other forces. Integration is used in two different senses: (a) shared meanings and (b) strong interpersonal relationships. Both can refer to properties of groups (e.g., highly integrated groups) and individuals (e.g., persons culturally similar to others or those with relationships in the group). It can predict the volume of suicides if misfortunes are equally likely in all societies, but it would not be possible, however, to predict individual instances of suicide from this explanation. Even though integration can refer to an individual level, its predictive value is limited, as only those who (a) experience a misfortune and (b) have a low degree of integration will commit suicide. There is no way from the theory to determine who will experience a misfortune. The origins of suicidal impulses are not related to integration. In addition, for Durkheim's theory to predict differences in suicide rates between groups, he must either assume a similar degree of misfortune among groups or assume that the forces of amplification were primarily responsible for determining the strength of suicidal impulses. In both cases, the theory could not predict which individuals in a loosely integrated group would take their lives because the primary impetus comes from misfortune, not integration. Durkheim says little concerning the role of society in creating misfortunes. An exception is found in his analysis of anomic and fatalistic suicide where the role of society is emphasized in creating individual suffering. Another hypothesis can be generated from this analysis:

HYPOTHESIS 3A: $nTm > (nIm)\ A = SR$

n = number of instances, Tm = magnitude of tragedy or misfortune,
Im = intensity of suicidal impulse, A = amplification factor, SR = suicide rate

Hypothesis 3A applies only at the group level and states that the frequency and intensity of misfortunes in a society will cause a certain number of persons to experience suicidal impulses with a range of intensities. It also indicates that a low SM/M (normative integration) or a high percentage of isolates (communicative integration) will increase the magnitude of suicidal impulses in the population. The qualifications stated above apply with respect to predicting suicide rates in a society, and no hypothesis could be generated at an individual level of analysis. An analogy is river of troubles; the slings and arrows of outrageous fortune, flowing through societies that have many strong social bonds will drag few over the abyss of suicide.

4. *Weakened Restraints*: This explanation views the role of society as neither a producer nor an amplifier of suicidal impulses, but rather as a restrainer of such impulses. It is not concerned with the origin of the suicidal impulse but views society's role of holding the impulse in check as primary. Whatever the sources of suicidal inclinations, groups differ in the degree of restraints they can exercise to check these individual impulses. Durkheim gave this explanation a secondary role as well. The amplification factor is a function of either SM/M or proportion of isolates in the population. Here again, two different definitions of integration are used by Durkheim: (a) integration as "shared culture" that controls the individual's behavior through norms and legitimate authority and (b) the "strength of the relational system" whereby the influence of the group is exerted on the individual through interpersonal relationships, obligations, responsibility, and the claims of others (Henry and Short 1954) from a strongly integrated group (or network of social relationships). Even though shared meanings can refer to both group and individual characteristics, no individual predictions can be made on this basis, because the origins of suicidal impulses are unconnected to integration. At the group level, Durkheim is asserting that Group A has a weaker system of norms and authority than Group B. Consequently, persons motivated toward suicide are more likely to be restrained in Group B than Group A. However, if Durkheim argues that groups with stronger restraints will have lower suicide rates, he must assume that there are similar proportions of persons with suicidal impulses in both groups and that the strength of the suicidal impulses in individuals are roughly the same in the two groups. Group B may have stronger restraints, but it may also have more people with suicidal impulses or stronger impulses. In this case, Group B would exhibit a higher rate of suicide than Group A even though it had stronger restraints. This explanation rests on the assumption that either there are similar proportions or impulses with similar degrees of intensity in different groups—perhaps a questionable assumption—or the strength of the resistance resulting from group integration is the only critical factor that need be considered in the suicide rate.

HYPOTHESIS 4A: $nib > (-R) = SR$

nib = number of persons with suicidal impulses of a certain magnitude,
R = resistance factor for a given society, SR = suicide rate

Hypothesis 4A states the suicide rate is primarily a function of the degree to which group restraints operate to check suicidal impulses. The amount of restraint is a function of either the degree of normative integration (percent shared meanings) or the strength of the relational system or communicative integration (percent isolates). In both Hypotheses 2A and 3A, nib may be constant and its inclusion in each case indicates that the SR is primarily a function of either amplification of suicidal impulses or resistance to suicidal impulses. Empirical research is necessary to test which factor was operative, as statistical analysis of rates would be identical under either hypothesis. Without independent investigation, it would not be possible to discern whether amplification or resistance was operating. Because there is no way to identify an individual as being prone to suicidal impulses from this perspective, no individual prediction could be made[9]. Furthermore, unless cultural dissimilarity was employed as the index, there would be no way of knowing which persons participated in shared meanings. If restraint evolves from the network of social relationships, then individuals with the fewest social ties would be the least subject to restraint or social control. Individual predictions could only be made in this instance if one could identify those with suicidal impulses. However, if one assumed similarity in suicidal impulses in both integrated and nonintegrated populations, then those most integrated would have the lowest suicide rates. An alternative is to view the strength of the barrier as being so strong that restraint is the significant factor regardless of the frequency or intensity of suicidal impulses in the group. In both cases, no individual predictions can be made. It would appear likely from Durkheim's analysis of the importance of social control in integration, his position would be that *weakened restraints are the critical element in egoistic suicides and individual predictions could not be made if this is the case.*

The four possibilities are as follows:

a Suicidal impulse—no resistance— suicide
b Suicidal impulse—resistance—no suicide
c No suicidal impulse—no resistance—no suicide
d No suicidal impulse—resistance—no suicide

Integration as Social Relationships or Interaction: Here, integration can refer to cohesion or the strength of the social bond that increases cohesion. Groups that have high rates of interaction or intimate relationships produce more meaning or provide more support. Those isolated from such interaction would be those most likely to commit suicide.

An Equilibrium Between Egoistic—Altruistic and Anomic—Fatalistic Forces: With Douglas's interpretation, it would not be possible to identify individual instances of suicide, as the concept only refers to group attributes. It also refers to equilibrium in the total society, not just subgroups.

Furthermore, it would not be possible to develop operational measures of "balance" or "equilibrium" other than by working back from the suicide rate. To use this ex-post facto measure as an explanation of the rates in society would be circular reasoning, and thus, the empirical fruitfulness of this concept is limited.

Summary: Of the different hypotheses Durkheim offers for why the lack of integration causes high suicide rates, only two had implications for predicting individual suicides, "individual sentiments of meaninglessness" and "collective sentiments of meaninglessness" but made opposite predictions. The "individual sentiments" hypothesis implied the least integrated Catholics would be most likely to take their life, and the "collective sentiments hypothesis implied the most integrated Catholics would take their life. With respect to the other hypotheses, no predictions about which individuals would take their life was possible. Thus, the answer to the question of whether Durkheim's theory predicts to individual egoistic suicides is—it *depends on what explanation is examined and the intervening variables that are involved in the explanation.*

Integrating macro/micro levels revealed aspects of the theory that have implications for individual egoistic suicides

Exploring linkages between macro and micro levels of analysis brought into sharper focus the processes by which the lack of integration generates suicides, the theory's ability to apply at the individual level, the contradictory predictions among the hypotheses, and the inability of variables like the "amplification of misfortunes" and "weakened restraints" to predict even rates of suicides without additional information such as the number of people with suicidal impulses and the relative strength of those impulses. Therefore, the hypotheses and theory are incomplete as they stand. Durkheim regarded individual and collective sentiments of meaninglessness as primary and weakened restraints and amplification of misfortunes as secondary in accounting for the volume of suicides.

In addition, some scholars suggest that "feelings of meaninglessness resulting from social differentiation" was the primary factor in Durkheim's early chapters of *Suicide* (1897) and therefore should be considered in predictions of individual suicides. However, in the later chapters, Durkheim speaks of "social currents" imposing somber views on persons, seemingly emphasizing the effects of "collective" sentiments of meaninglessness on individuals causing them to take their lives. Thus, internal contradictions in *Suicide* have to be reconciled. Individual predictions still depend on which chain of intervening variables is examined, as some analyses lead to individual predictions while others do not. The ones most likely to commit suicide in Hypothesis 2B, are those most integrated, but in Hypothesis 1B it is the least integrated. This suggests integration operates in different and conflicting ways in regard to suicide. These inconsistencies in Durkheim's theory have not been addressed and cause difficulty in interpreting the theory and inconsistent research findings in empirical studies.

For example, if feelings of "meaninglessness" cause individuals to take their life, and the least integrated are most subject to these feelings, then the theory can predict individual instances of suicide (Berk 2006). Here, it is the absence of society that generates the feelings of meaninglessness that lead to suicide, whereas if these feelings are imposed by the collective morality, and individuals most integrated are tightly bound by that morality, then they are the ones most subject to suicide. In the latter case, it is the presence of society which is disintegrating that causes suicide[10].

However, if integration is important primarily because it intensifies the impact misfortunes have on human suffering or on one's feelings of meaninglessness, which contribute to suicidal actions, then only those persons who both (a) experience a misfortune and (b) lack group support to mitigate the intensity of the misfortune or feeling, are subject to suicidal pressures. Individuals who are not integrated but who also did not suffer a misfortune or meaninglessness would not be likely to commit suicide. If there is not a way of predicting which individuals experience misfortunes or meaninglessness, then no predictions at the individual level could be made from the knowledge of only the degree of integration of the group. A similar conclusion would follow from conceiving of integration as a form of "restraint." To make individual predictions, one must have knowledge of who already has suicidal impulses and how strong they are.

Even if troubles are random, the amplification of their impact or the group's ability to restrain suicidal impulses may be the only critical factors shaping the volume of suicides in a society. Consequently, poorly integrated groups either cause or permit more suicide by the reduction of their preservative value by intensifying suffering during misfortunes or in failing to hold in check suicidal impulses. However, individual predictions still can be made even when it comes to intensification of misfortunes if the moral structure fails to keep individuals from succumbing to their feelings when the individual is not integrated into the group. The same would be true for those least integrated persons who would experience less restraint of suicidal impulses. But for individual predictions, knowledge of whether the individual has suffered a misfortune or has suicidal impulses must also be known.

Thus, making individual predictions requires knowledge of the preservative value the group offers plus the individual's experience of misfortunes or having suicidal impulses; however, the preservative value is tied to the social not the moral structure. When Durkheim discusses groups acting as shock absorbers intensifying or mitigating misfortunes, it is social relationships which provide the supportive structures adhering them to society to weather crises and misfortunes or to mitigate loneliness from the lack of social ties. When the social rather than the moral structure is the defining characteristic of integration, the individual's position in the social structure determines their vulnerability and therefore leads to individual predictions as to who is most exposed to the social forces causing egoistic suicide.

If misfortunes trigger suicide, Durkheim did not consider that societies may differentially produce misfortunes and problems for their members, other than those which were caused by the lack of integration or regulation.

However, Durkheim did not use the causal chain to determine if his theory could make predictions of individual suicidal acts. Our examination revealed some causal chains could predict individual instances of suicide. Unfortunately, Durkheim did not elaborate sufficiently on the causal linkages between the three other types of suicide and their causes, and therefore, we cannot determine whether they have individual implications or not.

Durkheim's efforts to link social causes to individual suicides

Durkheim's third and final objective in *Suicide* (1897) was to identify the relations between social causes and individual suicides. This is the least developed aspect of his theory and the one most ignored by scholars. Earlier effort at integrating macro with micro analysis revealed two hypothesis derived from Durkheim's inverse law that permitted individual predictions of suicide. The two hypotheses, however, made opposite predictions; one that the least integrated and in the other, the most integrated individuals were more likely to commit suicide. Unfortunately, Durkheim stopped short at this point in his analysis and did not pursue this avenue further before he turned his attention to the other causes of suicide.

Durkheim turned his attention to the problem of relating social causes to individual acts of suicide. However, his approach was more unfocused and sporadic throughout *Suicide* and was the least developed aspect of his theory. Durkheim did not believe either group differences or individual instances of suicide could be explained by investigating individual's motives because motives could not be taken at face value, and they also would not lead to the social causes. Because there are societies where suicides do not occur and therefore, there are no motives sufficiently powerful enough to cause anyone to take their life in those societies. Even when people have the same experiences or feelings that drove individuals in other societies to suicide, they do not kill themselves because in those societies no motive is sufficient to cause suicide. Conversely, in weakly integrated societies, like the U.S., almost anything could be a pretext for suicide, which wouldn't be a cause in more integrated societies. Thus, motives alone are insufficient to cause individuals to commit suicide. There must be something in the society, other than people with motives and desires to end their life, which produces suicide. And if this factor is already present in the society, it may not take any specific experiences, feelings, or motives to cause individuals to commit suicide. The pretext of the suicide may not be the sole cause or even an important factor in the suicide, as many persons facing the same predicaments in a different society, don't automatically commit suicide.

Durkheim clearly not only had an interest in linking social causes to individual suicides, but believed social causes were the underlying reasons for all suicides in society. He asserts in one place, "that the collective inclinations for... (suicide) ...(are)...the source of all individual inclination" (1952:xvi) and in another "The incidents of private life which seem to be the direct inspiration of suicide and are considered its determining causes are, in reality, only incidental causes" (1952:173). Durkheim makes this claim with little supporting evidence, nor does he tackle the issues related to it directly. However, whether Durkheim's overall theory involving all four types of suicide, has implications for individual predictions is unclear. We have already observed that *the relationships between macro and micro analysis are complex and the ability to make individual predictions depends on the theoretical formulation and causal linkages of the intervening variables.*

Durkheim utilizes micro analysis when he explores individual subtypes of suicide (1952:146). Macro theories can often be tested by examining micro implications that may exist. Only by identifying the underlying social mechanisms through which the variables accomplish their effects can the questions of "how" and "why" suicide occurs be answered. By investigating the causal nexus between integration and regulation and suicide rates, the meanings of Durkheim's theory, its ambiguities, incomplete specifications, and the alternative explanations contained within the theory, can be brought into focus. Disagreement exists over the theory's ability to predict individual instances of suicide. Robinson's (1950) "ecological fallacy" occurs as a result of inferring relations between variables for individuals from relationships between variables obtained from the aggregate. Some critics have leveled such accusations against Durkheim on the assumption that his theory was concerned with explaining the correlates of individual instances of suicide. Regardless of what position is taken with respect to the controversy of the applicability of the theory to individual instances, the criticism remains valid when leveled at Durkheim's arguments in discrediting insanity as a cause of suicide.

A second way Durkheim sought to link individual suicide to social causes is to pursue individual differences with respect to susceptibility to social currents. Though every society produces more individuals that are susceptible (neurotics, depressives, etc.) than take their life, the rate is a measure of the strength of the current or force and not a function of the number of susceptible individuals. It is ironic he suggests psychological vulnerability to social currents as a factor leading to suicide but alters it somewhat as he states that it is not the depression per se that causes suicide but the depression plus the social currents which result in suicide.

A third effort to link social causes to individual suicides was his observation that individual manifestations reflect the social causes of suicide (1952:146). Yet somewhat contradictorily, Durkheim also states that not all suicides were social. Some resulted solely from the person's own nature, and even in specific social types, victims give their act a personal stamp that expresses their temperament and the social conditions in which they are involved. Suicides resulting from social causes leave a shading and special marks expressive of the individual.

Egoistic suicides are acts devoid of passion, reflecting detachment, emptiness, and melancholy. There is an absence of violent passions. Empty indifference, withdrawal, and feelings of meaninglessness or melancholy will characterize the emotional state of the individual. Altruistic suicide, however, arises out of conviction, a sense of duty, accomplishment, or fulfillment. It is a decisive act. Anomic suicides result from strong passions such as anger, frustration, despair or disappointment. The individual is over excited, and it is often an immediate and impulsive act. Fatalistic suicide is characterized by futility.

The various forces may combine with each other creating blended types so that any particular case may manifest some of each of the influences. The overall rate in the group is a combination of all types that exist in the society, all flowing into the stream of suicides. Societies also vary in the favorite method of committing suicide, although this does not seem to vary with the type of suicide. The social causes individualized in us are complicated by various means depending on the personal temperament of the victim and the special circumstances in which they are to be found.

Research could examine suicide notes or medical reports from victim's statements to access emotions and examine if they differ between circumstances. During economic crises, there would be more expressions of frustration or despair than in comparison to stable times reflecting anomic forces. Whereas during times of social disintegration, feelings of meaninglessness or emptiness would be more apparent reflecting the decline in integration. Further investigation may reveal differences in positions in the social structure that are more likely exposed to the social currents that flow through the society.

These considerations suggest predicting individual suicides would be extremely complex. Studies that work backwards from individual suicides to construct the social currents by the types of suicide would also be difficult at best. Another way to tease out links between social causes and individual suicides would be to examine the points of contact of individuals with the various social currents or their position in the social structure, as the currents flow down the channels of social organization.

However, as already suggested, this is the least developed of Durkheim's analysis and his claims were not supported by his analyses.

Durkheim's efforts to link social causes to individual suicides is complicated by virtue of his sometimes connecting the origin to the social structure rather than the moral structure, making it more difficult to link the social causes with individual acts.

Many examples and explanations of how these social causes produce their effects are tied to the system of social interaction, social organization and the social structure rather than the moral system of society. For example, several statistical regularities Durkheim cites to support his conclusion that "suicide is socially caused," seemingly contradict his main thesis that the statistical patterns of suicide are primarily a product of the moral structure of society. One regularity was (i) the *stability in suicide rates* of each society from year to year. Durkheim argues that the rate remains stable while the population is continually changing proves the causes of suicide are to be found in society, not in the individuals that comprise society, but he does not offer a thorough explanation with adequate supporting data for why rates are stable. He states that a year is needed to produce the full degenerative effect because the conditions of social activity change in both intensity and direction according to the season. An annual period is required for the same combination of activities to reoccur. The bill for potential suicides is paid in annual installments because the collective current requires a certain amount of exposure to penetrate individuals (1952:289). This links stability in rates to social interaction rather than the moral structure. Also confronting the issue of stability in rates later, he focuses his explanation on the social organization and the manner of associations among individuals (1952:286) and speaks of a "collective current" causing the collective inclination flowing down the channels of social organization. In both statements, he asserts interaction is important primarily because it exposes individuals to those forces that can affect them, but he does not take it further to trace it to the cause of the forces. Seemingly, the intensity of forces determines the volume of suicides, but the *channels through which the forces flow determine which individuals are affected. These statements remain compatible with his thesis that the character of the moral structure determines the nature and strength of social forces and the volume of suicides establishing the contingent of voluntary deaths.*

However, he also links the fluctuations in suicide rates to the rhythm of social interaction, which is compatible with his thesis, but makes interaction patterns an important element in driving suicide rates. Yet, his theory does not include this apparently important factor even as an augmenting intervening variable. The importance of interaction in creating solidarity is elaborated in Durkheim's later work on religion where he explores the impact of interaction and rituals in strengthening the power of religious and moral beliefs and of society over the individual. This also reveals another important way society gains control over individual's behavior and is still compatible with his major thesis but signals that interaction must be considered in assessing the strength of social forces.

Durkheim's last objective was to identify the relation of social causes to individual suicides. Durkheim did not directly address the question of why one person rather than another within a group committed suicide and some might argue this should not be a concern for sociological theory. Though this objective was not fully pursued, Durkheim believed he could account for individual actions and stated:

> It is not mere metaphor to say of each human society that it has a greater or lesser aptitude for suicide...quite its own, *and (is) the source of all individual inclination... These tendencies of the whole social body, by affecting individuals, cause them to commit suicide. The private experiences usually thought to be the proximate causes of suicide have only the influence borrowed from the victim's moral predisposition, itself an echo of the moral state of society.*
>
> *(1952:263-64) (italics mine)*

He presents little evidence to support this claim.

In his analysis of individual suicides, Durkheim links them to social organization which influence the direction down which the forces flow and determine which individuals are affected. This still leaves room for the character of the moral structure to determine the nature and strength of social forces and volume of suicides establishing the contingent of voluntary deaths. This collective force remains a property of society, and is external to the members in the society, but cannot be measured by individual inclinations.

> The proper way to measure any element of a collective type is not to measure its magnitude within individual consciences and to take the average of them all. Rather, it is their sum that must be taken, Even this method of evaluation would be much below reality, for this would give us only the social sentiment reduced by all its losses through individuation.
>
> *(1952:284)*

The social organization or patterns of associations are the channels through which the current flows, and its overall configuration determines the magnitude of suicides, and its paths determine which persons are affected by the currents. Social organization, therefore, plays a role in who is more exposed to the forces and thus likely to commit suicide.

"It is very rare, if not impossible, for one of these currents to succeed in exerting such preponderant influence over all points of the society. It always reaches this degree of energy in the midst of restricted surroundings containing conditions especially favorable to its development. One or another social condition, occupation, or religious faith stimulates it more especially. This explains suicide's twofold character. When considered in its outer manifestations, it seems as though these were just a series of disconnected events; for it occurs at separated places without visible interrelations. Yet the sum of all these individual cases has its own unity and its own individuality, since the social suicide-rate is a distinctive trait of each collective personality. That is, though these particular environments where suicide occurs most frequently are separate from one another, dispersed in thousands of ways over the entire territory, they are nevertheless closely related; for they are parts of a single whole, organs of a single organism, as it were." (1952:287).[11]

This, of course, makes it exceedingly *difficult to develop a societal measurement of the force, tracing all the individual conditions in society, outside of using the overall volume of suicides as an index of the overall societal forces.*

With respect to which specific individuals take their lives, Durkheim believed that individuals also must be susceptible to social currents and suggested that the civilization that breeds the anomic and egoistic tendencies also produces delicate nervous systems particularly vulnerable to anomie and egoism. "Society, therefore, cannot lack the material for its needs, for it has, so to speak, kneaded it with its own hand" (1952:288). Thus, when exploring the question of which persons in a social environment are most likely to commit suicide, *Durkheim ironically reintroduces individual psychological susceptibility, rather than sociological vulnerability.*

> The role of individual factors in the origin of suicide can now be more precisely put. If, in a given moral environment, for example, in the same religious faith or in the same body of troops or in the same occupation, certain individuals are affected and certain others not, this is undoubtedly, in great part, because the formers' mental constitution, as elaborated by nature and events, offers less resistance to the suicidogenetic current. But though these conditions may share in determining the particular persons in whom this current becomes embodied, neither the special qualities nor the intensity of the current depend on these conditions. A given number of suicides is not found annually in a social group just because it contains a given number of neuropathic persons. Neuropathic conditions only cause the suicides to succumb with greater readiness to the current. Whence comes the great difference between the clinician's point of view and the sociologist's. The former confronts exclusively particular cases, isolated from one another. He establishes, very often, that the victim was either nervous or an alcoholic, and explains the act by one or the other of these psychopathic states. In a sense he is right; for if this person rather than his

> neighbors committed suicide, it is frequently for this reason. But in a general sense this motive does not cause people to kill themselves, *nor, especially, cause a definite number to kill themselves in each society in a definite period of time.* The productive cause of the phenomenon naturally escapes the observer of individuals only; for it lies outside individuals. To discover it, one must raise his point of view above individual suicides and perceive what gives them unity. It will be objected that if enough neurasthenics did not exist, social causes would not produce all their effects. But no society exists in which the various forms of nervous degeneration do not provide suicide with more than the necessary number of candidates. Only certain ones are called, if this manner of speech is permitted. These are the ones who through circumstances have been nearer the pessimistic currents and who consequently have felt their influence more completely.
>
> *(1952:288)*

This last statement suggests that those most touched by the social currents (i.e., those most integrated) would be the most subject to suicide, and susceptible persons will succumb first. Introducing psychological variables such as depression that suggest it is an independent cause of suicide overlooks Durkheim's conception that they are the ones most likely to be affected by the larger social forces and without these forces suicide may not occur within such individuals. Furthermore, social conditions as well as genetics modify biochemical processes in the body. Only comparative studies of societies where egoistic forces are weak will depressives have less suicide.

Notes

1 Farbero and Schneidman (1961) assert it is not the specific problems that cause suicidal feelings but the individual's attitude toward them. It is their feelings of helplessness or hopelessness about those problems or life that leads to despair, feelings of futility, and attempts to end their life. They claim individuals do not really want to die and their attempted suicide is a "cry for help" that often goes awry. Whereas Durkheim defines suicides as acts where individuals intend to die, he would suggest their theory is more relevant to attempted suicides. What people's intentions were might be impossible to determine post facto. Farbero and Schneidman also differ in how they trace the origin of these feelings of helplessness and hopelessness leading to desires to end their life to individual experiences of learned helplessness rather than to the larger social forces impinging on them.

2 This aspect of Durkheim's theory is grounded in a "sociology of knowledge" perspective. It asserts that certain patterns of culture (low integration) generate specific beliefs, feelings or ideas (life is meaningless, empty or has no purpose) in the society or group. This condition gives rise to movements in philosophy or literature such as nihilism or existentialism where life is viewed as devoid of meaning and suicide is an acceptable response. The roots of such worldviews are lodged in the social organization of society. This explanation resembles the

processes involved in altruistic suicide, though it occurs in weakly integrated societies, where people are conforming to moralities contributing to their suicide.

3 Integration, sufficient moral structure, restrains all desires contrary to society's expectations including ending one's life and abandoning one's duties to society, keeping the individual under society's control. In addition, the lack of sufficient moral structure to control the individual's conduct also generates sentiments of meaninglessness and purposelessness that independently motivate individuals to end their life.

4 Durkheim discusses the disintegration of society failing to attach individuals causing isolation and egoistic suicide (1952:245).

5 One must be wary of committing the ecological fallacy as well, in interpreting the meaning of the hypothesis to imply the least integrated persons are the ones most likely to commit suicide.

6 For more expansion on the various definitions of integration, see pages 121 to 136.

7 If integration referred to social relationships, then it would be the ties to family, religious, or political groups that was critical in predicting individual suicides.

8 If there is a relationship between the emergence of these collective sentiments and the social organization of society and its various channels of influence, then individual predictions may be possible based on individual's social positions in society.

9 Research on persons seeking help in suicide prevention programs could compare the suicide rates of those who have close relationships versus the degree their moral obligations to society to examine the impact of social relationships versus strong moral beliefs and obligations in restraining suicide. An alternative is to look at studies that survey suicidal feelings of various populations and then assess degree of integration and see if any relation to their suicide rate.

10 When he focuses on collective sentiments, his explanation of the process by which society generates suicide is similar to his explanation of altruistic suicide where society's presence requires or encourages suicide. An undeveloped aspect of Durkheim's theory is how society generates meaning and how meaning provides an incentive to live. Society's disintegration robs individuals of their meaning of life and should be contrasted with the views of other scholars who attempt to account for the lack of meaning (Frankl 1984; May 1977).

11 Abrutyn (2023) enunciates Cavan's social disorganization theory of suicide which incorporates elements of Durkheim's concept of integration such as powerful normative systems, strong social controls, and isolation at the meso level of organization rather than the overall society by comparing neighborhoods and rates of suicide.

5

CRITICAL EVALUATION OF DURKHEIM'S STUDY AND THEORY OF SUICIDE

Scholar's efforts to unify Durkheim's theory

Durkheim did not provide a coherent summary of the theory, identifying all its parts and how they are related to one another. Few have discussed why though some (Douglas 1967; Parsons 1949) have suggested he changed his approach or lost his way. We will suggest a third reason as we unpack Durkheim's theory shortly.

Yet, some scholars have gone forward unifying his theory despite the lack of an overall formulation of the theory by Durkheim. Unfortunately, they only incorporated his first goal of the theory, to explain variances in suicide rates. They failed to incorporate his efforts to identify the causal linkages between the social forces and suicide or to link the social forces with individual suicidal acts, neither of which was well developed in the book *Suicide*.

Some scholars (Lester 1992:388; Pescosolido and Georgianna 1989:34, 45; Breault and Barkey 1982; Pope 1976:14, 57; Heyns 1975; Douglas 1967) have interpreted his writings to reflect a synthesis by positing a U-shaped relationship between both integration and regulation and the overall suicide rate which would incorporate all four types of suicides. This suggests the "inverse" relationship Durkheim postulated between integration and suicide was limited to egoistic suicide in the early chapters in *Suicide* (1897), while the "U" shaped relation of both integration and regulation incorporates the three other types of suicide, altruistic, anomic and fatalistic, covered in the later chapters in the book.

This synthesis could be construed as the current "consensus view" of Durkheim's theory of suicide. It incorporates Durkheim's "inverse law" which

DOI: 10.4324/9781003669272-5

perhaps is limited to only the egoistic spectrum of integration but expands his formulation to include societies and groups on the more integrated and altruistic side of the spectrum of integration and is also applicable to the relationships between regulation and suicide rates, thereby subsuming all four types of suicide. Thus, this synthesis postulates a "U" shaped relationship between both integration and regulation and suicide rates. The extremes of both low and high integration and low and high regulation exhibit high rates of suicide. In their graph, there is an equilibrium point that exists between the extremes of integration and regulation that minimizes suicide in society. This "goldilocks" balance must be empirically determined. This equilibrium point is compatible with Durkheim's functional analysis of society as a social system.

Both extremes, societies and groups with insufficient and excessive degrees of integration manifest high rates of suicide and the base of the "U" represents the point at which the balance between insufficient and excessive integration minimizes suicides in society. However, the important differences in the manner by which the different degrees of integration cause suicide, which create the distinction between egoistic and altruistic suicide, are not revealed in this formulation.

This formulation implies there is an optimum amount of integration, an equilibrium point, which minimizes suicide in society and illustrates the notion of balance or homeostasis in Durkheim's functionalist perspective. Neither too much nor too little integration minimize suicides in society.

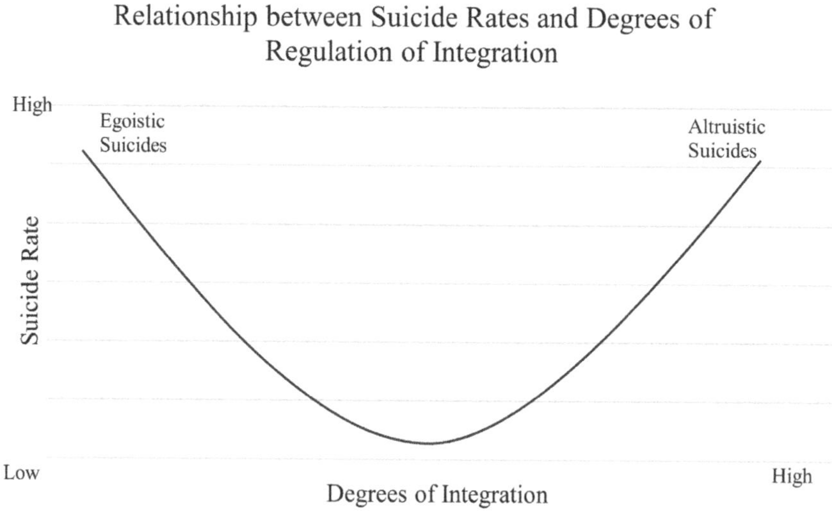

FIGURE 5.1 The formulation of Durkheim's theory, where both insufficient and excessive integration manifest high rates of suicide.

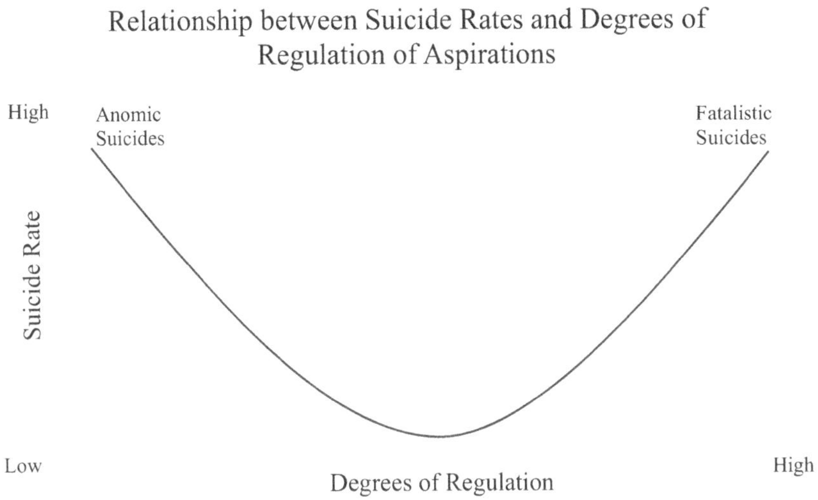

FIGURE 5.2 A similar analysis of the relation between levels of regulation and suicide rates. The extremes of regulation manifest high rates of suicide and where the optimum balance between a lack of sufficient regulation and excessive regulation lead to a point of regulation that minimizes suicide in society.

When degrees of integration can be precisely measured in quantitative terms, the nodal point, if one exists, can be empirically detected. This conceptualization reflects a shift from Durkheim's causal deterministic perspective to his functional perspective of society as a social system of interdependent parts in a moving equilibrium.

This formulation is the prevailing view of Durkheim's theory of suicide by many scholars in the field today. Next, we shall see why this is not an accurate depiction of Durkheim's theory, how this formulation fails to recognize numerous contradictions and incomplete specifications within the theory, and why Durkheim perhaps could not unify his theory.

A summary of Durkheim's theory to then identify obstacles in its unification

This section is not a unification of his theory, it is only a summary of it which reflects its disjointed nature. Any unification of his theory solely on these facts alone without expansion or revision will carry along with it the flaws of Durkheim's initial theory.

Let us summarize what Durkheim proposed and explore why he and others have been unable to unify his theory. We summarize Durkheim's work to reflect what can be firmly identified in *Suicide* in order to later identify reasons neither Durkheim nor others have been able to unify the theory.

Durkheim's study can be broken down into two parts. The first part of his study sets forth evidence to support his claim that suicide is socially caused. This aspect of the study has had an enormous effect on establishing sociology and illustrating a sociological perspective. To support the conclusion that suicide was socially caused, he cited several generalizations based on statistical regularities in the suicide rates that were already known by other scholars. He does not fully account for each of the regularities, only employing them to support the conclusion that suicide is socially caused. Once satisfactorily establishing that he had proved suicide was socially caused, the second part and main thrust of his study is to offer a sociological explanation and theory of suicide. His theory has three main objectives: (1) to identify the social causes of suicide, (2) to reveal the processes by which they cause suicides, and (3) to identify the relationship between the social causes and individual suicides. Another objective, though not explicitly stated, was to identify the origin of the social forces causing suicide in society.

1 The first part of Durkheim's study was to prove suicide was socially caused and he offered numerous *justifications for believing suicide is socially caused:*

   a The suicide rate is stable from year to year.
   b Each society has its own characteristic rate.
   c Each society has its own rate of acceleration.
   d Suicide rates fluctuate with changes in social organization.
   e Societies at similar technological levels have similar suicide rates.
   f Each subgroup in society has its own characteristic suicide rate.

These facts proved to Durkheim that suicide is socially caused and that at each moment in time every society had a definite aptitude for suicide.

2 *Durkheim's theory of suicide*:

The theory contains four parts. The first part identifies the factors in society responsible for creating the pattern of suicide and causing one society or group to have a higher rate of suicide than another—to identify the social causes of suicide. The second part explains how the social causes produce their effects. The third part of the theory traces the origin of the social forces causing suicide. The fourth and least developed part of his theory explores the relationship between social causes and individual instances of suicide.

Durkheim begins by identifying the nature of the social causes of suicide which he regards are social forces created by society. He detects the presence of social forces causing suicide by their manifestations in the statistical patterns of suicide.

(A) Durkheim's theory states the differences in suicide rates between societies and their different aptitudes for suicide result from differences in the strengths of two social forces, integration and regulation. These forces are generated by each society's moral structure. Integration refers to the degree to which the moral structure contains and constrains individual's behavior or the degree of control the society exercises over their members. Regulation refers to the degree to which the moral structure regulates individual's social appetites, so they are proportioned to the means available to individuals to satisfy those appetites in their social circumstances.

Extreme degrees of integration and regulation give rise to different social forces resulting in four distinct types of suicide. Egoistic suicides result from insufficient integration and altruistic suicides from an overabundance of integration, and anomic suicides from insufficient regulation and fatalistic suicides from excessive regulation. Each type of suicide reflects the social force that gives rise to them. Egoistic, anomic, and fatalistic suicides all result from the lack of sufficient attachment of individuals to society, whereas altruistic suicides result from excessive attachment to societies whose norms require or encourage suicide. Durkheim asserts the moral structure gives rise to the forces that attach members to society and regulate their social appetites, though the processes by which the two forces attach members are very different. Integration attaches people by extensive social control through powerful norms that regulate broad areas of social life, and regulation attaches individuals by satisfying an adequate level of their social appetites in their social conditions to motivate them to keep living. Thus, each type of suicide is caused by different social processes emanating from the different social conditions in society that give rise to them. The strength of each of the forces determines the volume of suicides generated by each society.

Durkheim noted certain regularities and patterns in suicide rates that indicate the presence of social forces. One is that suicides increase during industrialization and increase even more in advanced and richer countries where capitalism had emerged. Industrialization weakened the ability of modern society to integrate its members sufficiently into its social order giving rise to increasing suicides. He further noted that differences between religious, social, and political groups within societies also varied with the degree of integration of the group, prompting him to posit his "inverse law" of the relationship between degrees of integration and suicide rates and labeled the social force egoism. He then presented evidence supporting the law. He proceeded to identify three other social forces causing suicide: altruism, anomic, and fatalistic forces. However, Durkheim did not synthesize his conclusions about all four types of suicide in an overall set of propositions integrating how all the social forces were related to suicide rates.

(B) The second part of Durkheim's theory addresses the processes by which social causes produce suicides. Egoistic suicide results from the weakening of society's presence and control over the individual both (a) weakening the moral structure's ability to restrain any existing suicidal impulses and (b) creating feelings of meaninglessness and purposelessness as the moral structure diminishes, leading to suicidal sentiments and ultimately suicides. The disintegration of society's moral structure also produces "collective sentiments" of meaninglessness and purposelessness which are imposed upon members by society like other sentiments affecting individuals directly and causing suicides. In the first case of egoism, it is the absence of society that fails to restrain individual sentiments while in the second case of altruism it is the presence of society that produces these sentiments that lead to suicidal actions. Altruistic suicides occur in tightly knit societies characterized by excessive integration that have evolved norms demanding or encouraging suicide. These suicides result from society's strong presence in individual's lives and are acts of conformity affirming societal morality. Whereas in most egoistic suicides, individuals assume the right to take their life disregarding their obligations to society, and they are likely viewed as deviant or a threat to society. Egoistic suicides caused by collective sentiments resemble the process involved in altruistic suicides except in a weakly integrated group. In the absence of norms requiring or permitting suicide, altruistic societies don't necessarily have high rates of suicide. It is only certain types of altruistic suicides and one type of egoistic suicide, out of all types of suicide, which do not result from a lack of attachment to society.

Anomic suicide results from insufficient regulation of social appetites or desires. These increase during (a) economic fluctuations or crises, (b) increasing materialism and rising consumer capitalism, and (c) periods of rapid social change. The lack of regulation results in a proliferation of unchecked and unsatisfiable desires with the inevitable and unbearable frustration resulting in anomic suicides. Fatalistic suicides result from the opposite condition, where individual's desires are so thwarted by moral proscription and social conditions that cause unbearable frustration from unfulfilled desires leading to hopelessness and suicide. Fatalistic suicides are infrequent and found mostly in limited situations in modern society and are given little attention in *Suicide*. Both anomic and fatalistic suicides fail to attach individuals adequately to society by failing to provide sufficient gratification of their social appetites which lead to unbearable frustration and hopelessness. Capitalism also compromises the collective conscience's ability to control behavior and weakens integration through its encouragement of self-interest.

A society's location with respect to the dimensions of integration and regulation generates social forces whose strengths determine the volume and types of suicides that will occur in each society.

(C) The third part of the theory identifies the source or origin of the social forces causing suicide. Durkheim linked the origin of the forces to changes in the moral structure of society wrought by industrialization and specialization in the division of labor and less explicitly the development of materialism or capitalism which alters the value systems by emphasizing material acquisition, self-interest, and unrealistic expectations. Thus, the social change wrought by industrialization diminished and transformed the moral structure of society both weakening individual's attachment to society and creating social forces driving individuals to sever their relations with society by taking their lives. The evidence in support of the proposition that the forces emanate from changes in moral structure is largely contained in the *DLS* (1893) and less in *Suicide* (1897). These changes were seen to vary with changes in the suicide rates with the emergence of industrialization and the accumulation of wealth by society. He also traces the differences in suicide rates between religious groups to their moral structures, but his proof that the origin of the social forces is the moral structure is neither strong nor conclusive.

(D) The fourth and least developed aspect of Durkheim's theory deals with the relation of social causes to individual suicides. Durkheim asserts that the social causes (forces or currents) are the ultimate source of all suicides in society. However, he presents little evidence to support this claim. He also puzzlingly makes reference to idiosyncratic suicides in the work. However, when he explores the links between integration and suicide, if he had carried his analysis further, he would have found two hypotheses, implicit in the theory but unrecognized by Durkheim, which might have led closer to individual predictions. In one case of individual sentiments of meaninglessness, the least integrated were most likely to commit suicide. In the other case of collective sentiments of meaninglessness, the most integrated persons were most likely to commit suicide (Berk 2006). In addition, while exploring whether suicide was socially caused, Durkheim found those belonging to groups, the married versus single persons, and those from larger families, were less likely to commit suicide. From findings such as these, an actuarial table could be constructed increasing individual predictions.

Social causes also could be traced to individual reactions since each social current leaves its stamp on the suicide as well. Egoism results in an empty and detached feeling, whereas altruism generates prideful or shameful feelings or elation, while anomic forces create feelings characterized by frustration and fatalism by feelings of futility, despair or hopelessness. Each society may also leave its stamp by a particular method or ritual. Relevant data could be collected linking social causes to individual suicides but were not in his study. However, specific suicides may result from a blend of different forces somewhat complicating their identification. Having any social connections, such as being married, being a member of a large family, or being a part of other groups with high dynamic density inhibits suicide while their opposite increases suicides. As society's social glue weakens at the points of contact with individuals, suicides increase. Crises or threats against society may unify individuals and make them feel more a part of society and subsequently decrease suicides.

Critical evaluation of Durkheim's study and theory of suicide

Though Durkheim's classic treatise is an icon and one of the most significant pieces of sociological research undertaken in the last century, numerous problems remain in the theory. Subsequent research has not moved substantially beyond these incomplete and incorrect formulations of Durkheim's theory.

Premature rejection of non-social causes

First, Durkheim was *precipitous in his rejection of non-social causes* of suicide. He rejected all non-social explanations even though his analysis of non-social explanations was not exhaustive. Furthermore, in his attempt to discredit them, he *committed an error in reasoning, the ecological fallacy* (Robinson 1950); drawing conclusions about a relationship between two variables (insanity and suicide) in an individual person based on their statistical relation in an aggregate of persons (a correlation at a group level). He argued "if suicides were a function of insanity, they should occur more frequently among groups that had high rates of insanity." Females, therefore, should have higher suicide rates than males because of their higher rates of insanity, yet the opposite was true: suicide is essentially a male phenomenon. Therefore, his conclusion that suicide and insanity were unrelated was unwarranted. In addition, the term "insanity" is outdated, though measurement of mental illness remains problematic.

A common criticism of Durkheim's theory is that he prematurely rejected mental illness as a factor in suicide; however, in his analysis of the volume of suicides with which each society is afflicted, appeared unrelated to mental illness as rates remain stable while there was a turnover in the population of people who might have been mentally ill, so that the rate remained constant as variability in numbers of the mentally ill changed; however, the criticism might be more valid when directed toward which individual was likely to commit suicide. It is time for a reassessment of modern psychiatric and psychological theories of suicide and the related research studies. Do psychological, biological, or brain functioning variables have independent effects on suicide? Sociological research has demonstrated social structure and social processes cause stress and other reactions which create psychological vulnerabilities, biochemical imbalances, and patterns of brain functioning associated with depression, mental disorders, and suicide. Often psychological predispositions or brain disorders are believed to be caused by genetics. Yet, the importance of the environment and epigenetics in shaping the expression of genes is becoming increasingly clear. Research has shown how experiences can negatively affect even life in the womb having repercussions generations later. Harmful and long-lasting effects of social experience, like Adverse Childhood Experiences (ACE), on a wide range of disorders have been well documented. The role of class structure, community organization, ethnic, gender, and class discrimination in generating harmful effects on the body and mind, weathering effects, have been identified dating back to Faris and Dunham (1939) and Hollingshead and Redlich's (1958) classic studies. Even though there may be psychological vulnerability to the forces of suicide, these might be sociologically induced. Recent studies show relationships between depression and suicide, which have shed light on the role of serotonin and other neurotransmitters that need to be examined in suicide. The role social experiences play in altering the balance of biochemicals such as neurotransmitters also needs to be examined. Studies of brain development and functioning show the importance of social processes in the wiring and functioning of the human brain and need to be considered as independent factors and processes in the body and brain as the mechanisms by which social forces effect human behavior. Cross-cultural comparisons of individuals with psychological vulnerabilities could indicate whether the social forces are truly responsible for all suicides rather than individual vulnerabilities. Even if there was a relationship between depression and suicide, this does not necessarily mean that depression is the sole cause of suicide. It may simply place a person at a particularly vulnerable position to become subject to the social forces impelling individuals toward suicide. The chain of causation between the social forces, depression, and suicide has not been clearly explored. Depression may be the first consequence of social forces acting upon an individual, or it may be the result of individual circumstances that places a person at particular risk in becoming subject toward social forces impelling them toward suicide. The increasing use of antidepressants in the treatment of suicide prevention can inform us of the role biochemical processes play in suicides while also giving us an opportunity to examine the role of social factors in altering chemical processes in humans. Group differences in depression reveal that sociological variables also play a role in the creation of depression as well as suicide.

In addition to the premature rejection of non-social causes, four other generalizations were cited in support of the conclusion that suicide was socially caused, but Durkheim did not elaborate the linkage nor clearly relate it to the moral or social structures, though they were implied in the character of the generalizations.

Unreliable statistics

There are problems in using official statistics in the study of suicide in both their reliability and validity that taint most studies. Research in suicide prevention centers may permit collecting more precise information in determining if the relationships Durkheim proposes hold for those populations.

The validity of official statistics on suicide can be questioned: (a) Official statistics underrepresent the actual rate of suicide, as many are never detected and others are hidden to avoid shame, which may lead to systematic bias. (b) Furthermore, officials who create the statistics have no common agreement on the definition of suicide; certainly, it is not the same definition employed by Durkheim (Gibbs 1968:13). (c) Officials also have no clear method for determining whether a suicide has occurred. Suicide rates are thus dependent on the actions of the officials who create them, and as Douglas (1967:152–231) has shown, secular officials create different statistics than religious functionaries, though Pescosolido and Mendelson (1986) argue that this has little impact on the relationships between sociological variables. Definitions and determinations vary by district. They include the fact that the definition of suicide was problematical in regard to the official statistics of suicide, that official statistics were not gathered with Durkheim's definition in mind, and underrepresented the true rate of suicide due to some groups being reluctant to identify an individual act as suicide due to stigma. Third, Definitions varied by the functionary responsible, districts, societies, and historical periods.

Therefore, in regard to Durkheim's first project, proving suicide was socially caused, he gathered sufficient evidence to support that notion but more current research is needed. The conclusion he left with that section of the work was that the central question for sociologists is to account for the volume of suicides with which each society is afflicted. This task consumed the major part of *Suicide*, which is proposing a theory that supposedly could account for the central question of sociology and suicide. Next, we turn to the problems in his establishing a theory of suicide.

Failure to clearly define, operationalize, and measure independent variables

More conceptual clarity is needed in defining the independent variables and distinguishing them from each other. Had Durkheim not only made clearer what he meant by integration, for example, the several different definitions that have evolved associated with the theory would not have obscured what the theory implies. Had he developed operational definitions it would have provided those undertaking research to replicate and expand his analyses. Lastly, had he actually empirically measured integration he would have been able to assess his theory's ability to account for the volume of suicides with which each society is afflicted in addition to avoiding the misunderstandings and disputes that have arisen around this aspect of his theory. It also would have avoided arguments about whether integration and regulation were a separate or a singular force (Johnson 1965; Gibbs and Martin 1958). It also would have forced him to come to terms with which aspect of society, the moral or social structure generated the social forces and whether the social structure or social interaction, have to be taken into account as well as integration and regulation.

In addition, Durkheim made no attempt to measure the reliability and validity of his major concepts.

Different meanings of "integration" create ambiguity in Durkheim's theory

Durkheim failed to rigorously specify his independent variables, leaving ambiguities, conflicts, and gaps in both integration and regulation. With respect to integration, Durkheim never clearly defined nor developed an operational definition and never measured the degree of integration of various groups (Gibbs and Martin 1958, 1964; Stack 1983). Therefore, his conclusions about the relationship between integration and suicide are unsupported lacking any empirical measurement of the level of integration of religious confessions, marital conditions, and states of the polity. This shortcoming led to different interpretations of "integration" and consequently to considerable differences among scholars interpreting the theory. "Integration" has been used variously to refer to shared beliefs, social interaction, social relationships, social organization, feelings of cohesiveness, the vitality of society, and to the balance of egoistic and altruistic forces within a group. Thus, Durkheim's ambiguous and sometimes conflicting use of the term has led to several different referents for integration in the literature.

A Integration as a manifestation of the *moral structure* of society
"*Integration*" *as* "*Shared Beliefs and Practices.*" This definition most closely approximates Durkheim's intent to examine the role of the moral structure in creating cohesion in society and impacting suicide. Integration here refers to the system of norms, beliefs, and customs of the group—that is, to its culture. In his analysis of differences in suicide rates between religious confessions, Durkheim stressed the system of shared beliefs and practices as central:

> The only essential difference between Catholicism and Protestantism is the second permits free inquiry to a far greater degree than the first.
>
> *(1952:112)*

> Protestantism ... has fewer common practices . . . the more extensive is the credo the more unified and strong is the society.
>
> *(1952:113)*

> A religious society . . . (attaches) them completely to an identical body of doctrine . . . in proportion as the body is extensive and firm . . . Judaism . . . consists basically of a body of practices minutely governing all the details of life and leaving little free room to individual judgment.
>
> *(1952:114)*

> Religion protects man . . . because it is a society. What constitutes this society is the existence of a certain number of beliefs and practices common to all the faithful, traditional and thus obligatory. The more numerous and strong these collective states of mind are, the stronger the integration of the religious community, and also the greater its preservative value.
>
> *(1952:125)*

Similarly, Durkheim asserts: "the suicidal tendency is great in educated circles, this is due, as we have said, to the weakening of traditional beliefs and to the state of moral individualism resulting from this" (1952:123). Durkheim also examined the impact of the family, particularly the consanguineal unit, which like religious society has a preservative effect. Specifically with respect to the issue of density of the family, he argued:

> [The number of children] may be of no significance if they do not actually and consistently share in group life . . . the density of a group cannot sink without its vitality diminishing. Where collective sentiments are strong, it is because the force with which they affect each individual conscience is echoed in all the others, and reciprocally. The intensity they attain therefore depends on the number of consciences which react to them in common.
>
> *(1952:159)*

Consequently, in a family of small numbers,

> common sentiments . . . cannot be very intense, for there are not enough consciences in which they can be represented and reinforced by sharing them. No powerful traditions can be formed there as unite the members of a single group . . . Small families are also inevitably short-lived; and without duration no society can be stable. Not only are collective states weak . . ., but they cannot be numerous; for their number depends on the active interchange of views and impressions . . . In a sufficiently dense society, this circulation is uninterrupted; for some social units are always in contact . . . Likewise, when the family is small, few relatives are ever together; so that domestic life languishes ... But for a group to be said to have less common life than another means that it is less powerfully integrated; for the state of integration of a social aggregate can only

reflect the intensity of the collective life circulating in it" (1952:159-60). Durkheim is also asserting systems of social interaction with high social densities that strengthen moral beliefs and the power of groups over individuals[1].

Durkheim also explored the impact of crises and wars that "rouse collective sentiments, stimulate . . . patriotism, political and national faith, alike, concentrating activity toward a single end, at least temporarily cause a stronger integration of society" (1952:208). In Durkheim's analysis of religion, education, family, and the polity, the commonality of beliefs and practices is stressed as a manifestation of "integration." His analysis follows from his earlier conception of "mechanical solidarity" where cohesion results from sharing common norms, values, beliefs, and rituals. The larger the scope of these common values or beliefs, the more powerful the force exerted to bind individuals to one another and to the group. By contrast, the more a culture permits individual judgment, the less the force exerted by the system to dominate the lives of its members, and the fewer the strings that tie individuals to the group, and subsequently to life itself.

However, Durkheim never explicates the nature of social bonds or measures the degree of cohesion wrought by the various forces. He uses suicide as an example of a weakened social bond, which formed the basis of his interest in suicide. Homans (1950), Turner (1990), Collins (1988: Ch.6, 2005), and Scheff (1990, 1997) investigated social bonds and the role of micro processes in creating social cohesion but through social relationships rather than shared beliefs. Durkheim identifies common beliefs and practices as the essential aspect of integration and the more they pervade various aspects of the individual's life, and the greater the extent to which they regulate behavior, the greater the integration of the group. Adherence to norms is the hallmark of a strongly integrated society, whereas individual reflection or discussion with respect to action characterizes a loosely integrated group. In this normative sense, integration refers to the group's culture; it is indicated by the extent to which the culture is: shared, pervasive, strongly held, and a guide for behavior. *Durkheim does not focus on the content of norms*, just that they are shared and regulate behavior. Presumably, any shared norms cause a tightening of social bonds. Some scholars see a change in the importance of the content of norms in the later part of *Suicide* (1897) like Parsons (1949) and Douglas (1967).

Durkheim contributes to the confusion over the meaning of integration by equating it with *shared beliefs* in comparing religious group's suicide rates but with the *intensity of social interaction* when examining family size, and with *group membership* in comparing the rates of suicide of the married with those of single and divorced persons.

B Integration as an aspect of the *social structure* of society

"Integration" as "Social Interaction." Some apparent confusion resulted when Durkheim discusses integration as it is related to family size, he focuses on social interaction as a key variable. He states that the intensity and vitality of a family is a function of increased interaction among the members—an augmentation associated with greater family size and increased social density. Social interaction re-establishes the sense of the collectivity and its authority, thereby intensifying common understandings and tightening social bonds. He also discusses increases in social interaction as responsible for increased suicide in warmer weather as it intensifies the effects of social life and cultural understandings. Gibbs and Martin (1958, 1964) in this vein, interpret "integration" to refer to social relationships and "the suicide rate of a population varies inversely with the stability and durability of social relationships within that population" (1958:141), but the volume, frequency, or intimacy of the interaction were not considered. Durkheim uses "social bond" to refer to strict social control by society and infrequently to social relationships. However, Durkheim found interaction in family density important *only because it increased intensity of the common sentiments.* "Consequently, in a family of small numbers of common sentiments cannot be very intense, for there are not consciences in which they can be represented and reinforced by sharing them" (1952:159).

The only justification for Gibbs and Martin's interpretation exists in Durkheim's discussion of the role of "mutual moral support" as a key element in *Suicide* (1952:168). At the support level, social interaction is crucial to diminishing shocks from society[2]. The same could be argued about loneliness and social isolation creating suicidal impulses. But Durkheim fails to recognize he includes aspects of social structure along with the moral structure perhaps because he considers these to be of secondary importance or they are inextricably intertwined. Even when discussing the restraining aspects of marriage in suicide, he emphasizes the importance of the institutional features of marriage and the social authority invested in the marital union as primary rather than the interpersonal relationship between the husband and the wife. What matters is that regulation should be accepted by the conscience, otherwise it has no moral authority. It chafes without accomplishing much (1952:232). *Durkheim continually emphasizes the primacy of culture over social relationships or social interaction.* Durkheim lacked clarity in distinguishing defining characteristics of "integration" from factors that increase integration and failing to distinguish culture from social organization or interaction by using the concept of "integration" to refer to both aspects of group life[3].

Pescosolido and Georgianna (1989) in a thoughtful reformulation of the role of religion in suicide also focus on social relationships as the basis for both integration and regulation. They state that "moral rules must be backed by a cohesive community to endure . . . We do not dismiss the importance of beliefs nor claim a causal ordering between beliefs and networks" (1989:40). However, they do not determine the relative contribution of social ties versus shared beliefs to variance in the suicide rates. Pescosolido and Georgianna (1989) supplant Durkheim's formulations with network analysis and *replace the concept of society with networks. Durkheim's emphasis was on the reality of society as sui generis and emergent, and the powerful force of the collective conscience and culture rather than social connections.* The role of social interaction was augmentry rather than a primary determinant of suicide. Pescosolido does suggest that continued interaction is essential to render beliefs strong and viable and that cultural configurations must be continually sustained and renewed by social interaction but places the primary emphasis on social relationships.

Stack's (1980) finding that divorce was more important than religion, Travis's (1990) finding that social isolation was more predictive than social disorganization, and Giddens's, (1972) association of social isolation, depression, and suicide all support a network rather than a cultural definition of integration. It is a question of whether ambiguity in Durkheim's theory created these inconsistencies or if they represent an alternative explanation. Research contrasting the relative contribution of social control (the degree beliefs are shared and regulate behavior) versus social networks (interaction and relationships) must be undertaken. Pescosolido and Georgianna, outside of church attendance, do not measure the richness of the social networks and infer them only indirectly; in the same fashion, Durkheim presents no empirical data that Catholics have more similar beliefs than Protestants. Durkheim was aware of the contexts of religious organizations and examined variance within denominations by comparing the Church of England, which is organizationally similar to the Catholic Church, with other Protestant denominations, and examining the minority status of a religious group in different societal contexts. Pescosolido's work points to the importance and interrelatedness of both macro structures and micro processes in the analysis of suicide. Mutual support performs integrative functions for social structures. Social relationships, they assert, also act as restraints (in anomic suicides). However, Durkheim focused solely on the "restraint of aspirations" from normative control rather than the restraints implicit in social relationships as the primary determinant of anomic suicide. Henry and Short's (1954) analysis of suicide also focused on the strength of external control through relationships rather than by norms. There are real differences between Durkheim's and Pescosolido's theories that need to be empirically examined[4].

Micro analysis can also reveal underlying dynamics of theories and flesh out the implications of the macro differences. Landecker (1950) identified several types of integration and distinguished "normative" (i.e., moral) from "communicative" (social) integration, a distinction Durkheim failed to recognize. Douglas noted a similar confusion in Durkheim's analysis of the primacy of "internal" versus "external" causes of social behavior (1967:47–51).

C Integration as balance of normative forces

"Integration" as "A Balance of Opposing Forces"

Douglas (1967) similarly argues that Durkheim did not use "integration" consistently; in the early chapters it referred to "shared meanings" but in the later chapters to "an equilibrium of opposing forces (egoism and altruism)." Douglas identifies three possible interpretations of integration: (a) the number of shared meanings; (b) the dimension of egoism–altruism, i.e., of noninvolvement or involvement in society; and (c) the equilibrium of the two opposing forces of egoism and altruism (1967:54).

Interpretation (a) implies any shared meaning, inasmuch as it constitutes a form of social regulation, can act to restrain suicide, which appears to be Durkheim's primary use of integration. Douglas rejects this interpretation in light of the larger meaning of Durkheim's work. (b) Egoism or altruism can also seem to refer to specific sets of moral beliefs that foster aloofness, involvement, or submission to society, which Douglas also rejects as he regards egoism or altruism as *orientations* to the primary social (moral) meanings rather than to specific social meanings as Durkheim ignored the content of the moral beliefs as a factor contributing to integration. The "cult of individualism" could be an exception to Douglas's analysis, where Durkheim linked the content of norms to altruistic suicide and identified specific norms requiring suicide. (Also see Pope 1976:34-38.) In egoistic suicide, noninvolvement in group life emerges from the lack of shared beliefs rather than from specific norms. Societies also form collective judgments about the value of life or individualism, but, according to Durkheim, these were epiphenomenal and evolved from the lack of shared beliefs (low integration). Once in existence, however, such collective representations can reinforce individual feelings of meaninglessness, thereby intensifying suicidal impulses in individuals, but have only a secondary reinforcing effect on decreasing involvement in society. These collective representations, when out of balance, exert a force upon the individual that produces individual states (such as melancholy) which, in turn, cause suicide if individual representations are not strong enough to contradict the force of collective representation. (1967:54) In his third interpretation, (c), Douglas asserts that the larger meaning of Durkheim's formulation should be extended to apply to the equilibrium of the opposing forces of anomie-fatalism, as well as to the balance of the two opposing dimensions of egoism-altruism and anomie-fatalism to achieve an overall equilibrium in society. Egoism and altruism are not specific sets of morals, but orientations toward moral meanings that constitute society, and represent the general orientations of submissiveness, aloofness, and rebelliousness—all of which are necessary for adequate functioning of any group.

> But an imbalance or upset in the equilibrium between the three leads to certain individual states in a certain proportion of the individuals in the group and thence to a given suicide rate[5]. Each force when not restrained by the other forces leads to suicidogenic forces within individuals.
>
> *(Douglas 1967:53)*

Durkheim may have changed his conception of the causes of suicide as Parsons (1949) contends, or Douglas's attempt to systematize the theory may have bent the meaning of integration, cohesion, and strength of social bonds to an unrecognizable form (a balance in the society of opposing forces).

There are problems with Douglas's interpretations. (a) If integration refers to a "balance" between two opposing forces, how could an inverse relationship between suicide and integration exist as Durkheim postulates? (b) Some have sought to unify egoism and altruism by positing a "U"-shaped relationship between integration and suicide where both high and low degrees of integration are associated with high rates of suicide and an optimum balance between them minimizes suicide rates. Although this interpretation is commonly found in the literature (Lester 1992:388; Pescosolido and Georgianna 1989:34, 45; Breault and Barkey 1982; Pope 1976:14, 57; Heyns 1975; Douglas 1967), it is not in accord with Durkheim's theory of altruistic suicide. High levels of integration do not automatically produce high rates of suicide. Altruistic suicide occurs in highly integrated societies only when there are specific norms requiring individuals to take their lives. Highly integrated societies that did not make suicide obligatory were not necessarily characterized by high rates of suicide. In contrast, low degrees of integration always generate high rates of suicide. This is one reason for the inconsistent findings with respect to religion and suicide rates. Findings on highly integrated religious groups and suicide are inconsistent and would only be expected to be high among religious groups that required such sacrifices or where the likelihood of group condemnation from failure or shame was also high. Durkheim's analysis of altruistic suicide was also more directed toward identifying the different forms, processes, and causes of suicide than in predicting actual suicide rates. However, his comparison of suicides in the army with those among the civilian population clouds the issue. Nonetheless, a "U"-shaped function or equilibrium conception is not in accord with the theory. Lester also suggested that little attention has been given to whether specific measures of integration and regulation are valid (1989:237). The link between the empirical variables employed in specific studies and the theoretical concept of integration is often tenuous.

(c) Douglas's interpretations rest on the belief that egoism-altruism and anomie-fatalism are interrelated and act as a force upon each other, and integration refers to a balance between the two dimensions. This would imply that a tightly knit society that requires suicide is somehow not integrated, contrary to Durkheim's conclusion. Durkheim viewed these dimensions as unrelated: egoism-altruism refers to the commonality of social meanings and the degree to which they regulate conduct, whereas anomie-fatalism refers to the degree to which norms regulate aspirations—dimensions that are independent of each other. Given there is no interdependence of the two dimensions, there is little justification for Douglas extending "integration" to refer to an overall equilibrium. There is perhaps some limited justification for Douglas's position in the later part of *Suicide* where Durkheim states:

> No moral idea exists which does not combine in proportions varying with the society involved, egoism, altruism, and a certain anomy. For social life assumes both that the individual has a certain personality, that [they are] ready to surrender it if the community requires, and finally, that [they are] to a certain degree sensitive to ideas of progress. This is why there are no people among whom these three currents of opinion do not co-exist, bending [people's] inclinations in three different and even opposing directions. Where they offset one another, the moral agent is in a state of equilibrium which shelters [them] against any thought of suicide. But let one of them exceed a certain strength to the detriment of the others, and as it becomes individualized, it also becomes suicidogenic, for the reasons assigned.
>
> *(1952:285)*

Durkheim distinguished "integration" from "equilibrium"—the former referring to the cohesive aspects of society resulting from shared social meanings and the latter to a state of organization in society that minimizes suicide. When Douglas equates these two concepts, he creates further confusion as well as glossing over the different processes at work that produce different forms of suicide. Although integration plays a role in both egoistic and altruistic suicide, its role is very different in eliciting the two forms of suicide. The substitution of "equilibrium" for "integration" leads to a belief that a synthesis has taken place when there is evidence that Durkheim had quite different notions regarding the causes of suicide that cannot be synthesized, as Douglas might suppose by changing the meaning of a term[6].

D Integration as organization or unity

"Integration" as "Organization" or "Unity." Landecker (1950) used "integration" to refer to unification or unifying processes; organization and unity are the key elements of integration. It can also refer to the organization of "smaller units into larger wholes," a part to whole analysis. Landecker further

specified types of elements that could be unified: cultural standards, behaviors, and persons. Three types of integration were derived from the combination of these elements though not all logical combinations were explored, or was logical consistency maintained in his analysis. "Cultural" integration referred to the degree to which cultural standards were consistent with one another which was similar to Linton (1936:282) definition of "integration" as the proportion of alternatives to universals and specialties. The lower the proportion of alternatives, the higher the cultural integration. "Normative" integration refers to the degree to which a person's behaviors were consistent with the cultural standards. "Communicative" integration referred to the degree to which interaction occurred with respect to cultural meanings (similar to Gibbs and Martin, 1964). Landecker believed social isolation was the primary cause of egoistic suicide, whereas Durkheim gave social isolation importance only because it decreases normative integration[7]. Landecker focused on the "unification process," which is related to the concept of "system," whereas Durkheim's concept of integration was linked to "cohesion" and "social bonds" resulting from extensive social control by the moral system. On the one hand, Durkheim was concerned with how systems are held together, and on the other hand, more importantly, the "extent the individual's behavior was regulated by the group—how social systems control behavior." Landecker's focus was on "systemic" properties, whereas Durkheim's was on social control and its contribution to cohesion. Durkheim explored social bonds in *The Division of Labor*, identifying two bases of social cohesion: mechanical and organic solidarity. Organic solidarity refers to cohesion resulting from mutual dependence fostered by the division of labor. Except that it purportedly decreased mechanical solidarity, this type of bond was of little concern in his analysis of egoistic suicide. However, mechanical solidarity, where persons are bound together by their common sentiments, formed the core of his conception of integration used in his analysis of egoistic suicide. Durkheim did not believe the cohesiveness wrought by functional integration was sufficient or of the right character to reduce suicide in a group. Douglas ignores cohesion and social control, factors that Durkheim considered crucial. Douglas's attempt to substitute "equilibrium" for "integration" merely focuses on the balance of submissiveness, aloofness, and rebelliousness without directing attention to the forces in society that produce cohesion.

E Integration as attunement

"*Integration*" *as* "*Attunement*" *or* "*Intersubjectivity*." The most micro theory of integration has been offered by Scheff (1997) and is not applicable on a societal level. His approach defines social solidarity in terms of "attunement" or intersubjectivity. This approach is parallel, but more clearly defined, than Durkheim's idea of "collective conscience," which refers to both conscience and consciousness. In Scheff's definition of solidarity, individuals can momentarily share beliefs and feelings collectively; they literally share a collective consciousness be it religious or political beliefs, on the one hand, or collective emotions like grief or anger, on the other[8]. Scheff outlines three basic degrees of collective consciousness: isolation (little or no shared beliefs/feelings), engulfment (little or no individual identity apart from the group), and solidarity (a balance between collective and autonomous individual consciousness). In his analysis, isolation is the basis for egoistic-anomic suicide, and engulfment is the basis for fatalistic-altruistic suicide. The isolated person feels alone in the world, to the extent that life may not seem worth living. The engulfed person has lost his or her individual identity, so the person's own life means little. Scheff's analysis opens the door beyond whether there are social connections, but the quality of the connection with others is as critical as the existence of a social connection and will be explored later.

Summary: At least five different definitions of "integration" can be identified in the literature associated with Durkheim's theory: (a) shared beliefs and practices; (b) social interaction; (c) a balance of opposing forces such as egoism-altruism and anomie-fatalism; (d) organization/unity; and (e) attunement. Other terms equated with "integration" such as "feelings of cohesiveness" or the "vitality of a group" employed by Durkheim can be viewed as consequences of integration and not a part of the meaning of that term. Thus, cohesion and control form the basis of Durkheim's conception of "integration." The strength of social bonds is a function of the degree to which collective sentiments are shared, pervasive, and serve as a guide to behavior. Intense interaction can increase the strength of the normative system to regulate behavior. A sequence demonstrating the consequences of low social interaction may be conceived as follows: low social interaction> few shared meanings and weak in regulating conduct>weak social bonds> high suicide (egoistic). Durkheim is referring to the degree to which society regulates individuals conduct (the amount of nonconformity would be a negative index), and the number and strength of shared meanings increases the likelihood of conformity to the normative system. Other factors enhancing social control such as effective societal reaction or high levels of surveillance by others in the community can also play a role in how much control society can exercise over individual behavior to influence suicide rates. Durkheim did not seem to believe the cohesiveness wrought by functional integration, organic solidarity, was relevant to suicide and therefore was of no concern in his analysis of egoistic suicide[9]. Although, we see an analogous process bonding individuals to society under the concept of regulation.

Mechanical solidarity, where persons are bound together by their common sentiments, formed the core of his conception of integration in his analysis of egoistic suicide. Not only does "integration" have different meanings, but it can also refer to different units and levels of analysis. Sometimes, the unit refers to properties of a group and other times to properties at the individual level. Different levels of abstraction are often involved in different types of integration. Douglas's concept of integration, a balance of opposing forces, is conceived at the societal level. Social relationships can apply at the individual as well as the collective level. This creates problems in the determination of integration because subgroups within a society may be tightly knit, whereas cleavages or conflicts exist at a societal level. Other terms equated with "integration" by Durkheim such as "feelings of cohesiveness" or the "vitality of a group" can be viewed as consequences of integration and not a part of the meaning of that term.

Durkheim's lack of clarity in defining integration, his failure to operationalize and undertake measurements of integration, his confusion of definitional components with both the causes and consequences of integration (equating integration with "feelings of cohesiveness" or the "vitality of a group when they are consequences of integration), and his use of the same term to refer to different aspects of group life (shared norms, interaction, social structure) have all contributed to the confusion surrounding this concept, his theory, and the different role integration plays in egoistic and altruistic suicide."

Different meanings of "regulation" also create ambiguity in Durkheim's theory

One of the complications of Durkheim's theory was a failure to sufficiently explicate the concept of regulation and fully develop his conception of anomic and fatalistic suicides. While Durkheim states regulation clearly refers to the degree of constraint by the norms of people's social appetites, anomic suicide is an example of the failure of adequately constrained appetites, and Durkheim identifies two conditions that give rise to anomic suicide, the inculcation of limitless desires or unquenchable appetites resulting from materialism or capitalism and the absence or failure of norms to constrain appetites such as periods of rapid social change or crises. The difficulty lies in his failure to describe fatalistic suicide as a consequence of overly restrictive norms alone. For example, he regards poverty as a constraint due to the social and economic organization of society, not overly restrictive norms. Slaves are overly constrained by virtue of their social status in society not by overly restrictive norms. The examples that one can mostly think of seem to be ones where the organization of society, its social structure, and capacity to produce the social rewards are most often the constraints one can imagine with regard to fatalistic suicide. One example resulting from norms may be over-emphasis of asceticism within early Christianity. Though through conforming to these ascetic norms, other appetites could be satisfied like respect, acceptance, or influence. This is perhaps why Merton formulated anomie as a consequence largely of goal disjunction, the social structure limiting people's opportunities. Therefore, is it accurate to state that fatalistic suicide is a result of over-regulation? This is a contradiction that needs to be resolved in Durkheim's theory; however, if Durkheim resolved this contradiction, he would not have the symmetry in his theory he may have sought. Merton addresses the issue somewhat when he talks about the relative emphasis of goals over means. He sees means or norms as legitimate avenues by which goals can be pursued, and that if only the goals are emphasized, the means will be trampled on and society will become a war of all against all, which reflects his focus on social order. So, in Merton's terms, the question would be: are there norms that would preclude ever achieving the goals? Durkheim did not sufficiently spell out the connections between insufficient and excessive constraint and the introduction of the concept of balance need to be further elaborated and specified. Durkheim's discussion of fatalism particularly but also anomie is incomplete with regard to resolving theoretical understanding.

Measurement problems

Similar problems previously stated in the analysis of Durkheim's use of official statistics continue to haunt his theory. In addition, Durkheim did not operationally define or empirically measure the degree of integration of any social group or society. His case rests largely upon argumentation. For example, he argued that Catholics are more integrated than Protestants but did not measure either their cultural homogeneity, level of conformity, or the character of their social relations, nor did he present data that Jews were more highly integrated than Catholics or Protestants. Nor did he operationally define or measure regulation in any group, society, or period of time and show it varied with suicide rates.

First, Durkheim's reliance on official statistics of suicide presents a serious drawback in his study. First, Catholics may not necessarily have a lower rate of suicide, but because of the stigma attached to it make more of an effort to cover up suicide when it occurs. Measures of reliability and validity of the official statistics were never undertaken by Durkheim and probably vary significantly by society.

Second, the determination of suicide is also more problematical than Durkheim acknowledges. A source of variance would be whether or not officials employ the same definition as Durkheim would in defining if a particular act were suicide.

Third, statistics are generated by official agencies. The number of such persons assigned to collect these data might influence the number of suicides detected. An increase in officials in technologically developed countries and more desire to detect possible suicides may alone account for the rate of acceleration of suicides.

Many scholars regard official statistics to be highly unreliable in this area. Measures of validity and reliability are lacking in both suicide rates and the two main independent variables of integration and regulation. Testing his theory rigorously would involve identifying types of suicide; however, it is exceedingly difficult to do so.

Problems with Durkheim's analysis of the data

Another problem is that even though Durkheim was far ahead of his time in the use of statistics, we must judge his work by current standards which illustrate numerous problems in his analysis of the data. Pope (1976) not only questions the validity of the facts upon which the theory rests but asserts that Durkheim selectively presented only those facts that agreed with his hypotheses and selectively omitted that which contradicted the hypotheses, incorrectly interpreted the statistics, switched definitions to fit his preconceptions, and failed to control for relevant variables. Durkheim failed to explore suppressor variables that might produce spurious non-correlations. Even his own data showed some relationships between mental illness and the suicide rate but were ignored by Durkheim. Furthermore, that he did not exercise proper controls and had he done this, many of the asserted relationships would have disappeared. That is, certain relationships might make it appear that no relationships exist between non-social variables and the suicide rate, which mask a relationship until examined more closely. For example, economic differences between Catholics and Protestants or in the size of family and suicide rate were not controlled in his comparisons.

Another concern is that Durkheim's theory only accounted for a small percentage of the variance, while other variables like sex, age, and race manifested very large differences. Yet he chose to ignore their importance. More advanced models exist to take into account the additional variables that need to be considered, such as the character of the normative system in highly integrated societies or the degree of goal disjunction or opportunities available in the social context in altruistic and fatalistic suicides.

Careful analysis of his data and later studies showed differences between Protestants and Catholics to vanish, and economic factors and industrialization or modernization explained more of the variance in his data.

Testing the hypothesis

It has been argued that Durkheim's use of data is more illustrative than a test of his theory and his rhetoric was more convincing than his data.

In the analysis of religious differences, he did not demonstrate that integration was the critical factor. For example, he could have examined individual's beliefs and their church attendance to distinguish cultural factors from actual practice of religion (see Pescosolido and Mendelson, (1986) for a network analysis). Did he show that Protestants exhibit more disillusion and despair than Catholics? Pope (1976) has argued that even his data did not show that Protestants have, in fact, a higher rate than Catholics. In any case, he did not control for other variables in his analysis of religious differences.

In the analysis of data, Durkheim frequently failed to control for the effects of other variables on the relationships he examined. When he compared Catholic with Protestant countries and attributed differences to religious factors, he did not consider that Catholic countries are also poorer, less industrialized, etc., and may explain more of the variance than religion. He fails to control for religious traditionalism when he examines the relationship of sex or education to suicide. In his analysis of religion, he also should have examined marital status, so that single Catholics could be compared with single Protestants.

Durkheim did employ specification of some relationships through the introduction of age as the test factor and constructed a four variable table where age, sex, and marital status were taken into consideration. This could be viewed as a progressive introduction of additional variables, where each is incorporated into the preceding analysis. Given the level of statistical sophistication at that time, Durkheim was employing advanced tools of analysis for social science.

Durkheim's theory does not explain all the regularities he identified in suicide rates such as: the total volume of suicides, the rate of acceleration in the rates, or differences in rates among various roles in society with the exception of gender roles.

Another serious problem with regard to testing Durkheim's theory is that he never undertakes a rigorous test of the proposition that these forces are generated by the moral structure. In fact, many of the links he makes to suicide rates are to systems of interaction, social structure, and social organization rather than to the moral structure. Neither links were empirically tested by Durkheim. Subsequent research (Simpson and Conklin 1989; Breault and Barkey 1982; Danigelies and Pope 1979; Stack 1978, 1980) has shown inconsistent support for Durkheim's conclusions.

Durkheim did not systematically incorporate his six reasonings for suicide to be a social act into his theory of suicide. This may have led to his failure to include the organization of society and social structure as sources of the social forces causing suicide. In regard to testing his theory of how social forces cause suicide, his theory was incomplete in articulating the intervening variables or causal nexuses that would have made it possible to understand how the social forces create suicide and thus test whether his theory could accurately predict individual suicides.

Did Durkheim lose sight of or change his objectives during the study?

How well did Durkheim accomplish his objectives? One issue that has never been clearly resolved is whether Durkheim saw his study as an attempt to answer the central question sociologists must in any theory of suicide. Durkheim asserts the central task for sociology is to explain the volume of suicides with which each society is afflicted. Durkheim did not address that question. Did he lose sight of that objective or did he change his objectives for *Suicide*? One reason pointing to him losing his way is that he did not measure integration and therefore could not determine how much each increment of integration contributed to the volume of suicides. This was also true of regulation. His failure to empirically measure and quantify the independent variables prohibited his ability to determine the volume of suicides associated with various degrees of integration and regulation. His stated objectives for his theory of suicide were (a) to identify the nature of the social causes of suicide; (b) to show how these causes produce their effects, and (c) to identify the relation of social causes to individual acts of suicide (1952:li). Instead of identifying the social forces holding society together, Durkheim focused largely on trying to account for the variances in suicide rates.

Instead of pursuing these objectives, he altered his focus to identifying why one society or group had a higher rate than another. Some charge that Durkheim became more concerned with explaining variations in suicide rates than with testing hypotheses about social cohesion. Others claim there was a dramatic shift in his approach in the early chapters from the later ones (Parsons 1949; Douglas 1967) but their claims were not well documented.

Durkheim lost continuity in his analysis of suicide throughout the study. He began identifying egoism as a cause in comparing the suicide rates of different religious, marital, and political states, connecting them to differences in moral structures. Then, when he undertook analysis of altruism, he did not compare the differences in rates of groups that were less integrated but focused mainly on the difference in the ways low integration caused suicide from how highly integrated groups produced suicide. He did look at differences in suicide rates with changes in economic conditions and how groups most tied to economic aspects were more affected than other groups but did not focus on differences in periods of rapid social change. But when it came to fatalistic suicide, he did little by way of analysis only citing some examples of the act. The fact that Durkheim never summarized the theory might suggest that there remained many unresolved issues that caused it to not fit well together.

Why the "consensus model" does not reflect Durkheim's theory

The first problem with the consensus model is that it does not take into account the problematical nature of Durkheim's formulation of the relationship between integration and suicide. In the first part of *Suicide*, where Durkheim offered his proof that suicide was socially caused, he used official statistics which counted all suicides as the same. Then later, he began differentiating them into the four types based on the different social conditions and social processes that gave rise to them. This led to confusion.

In the chapter on egoistic suicide, he posits his inverse law. The overall relationship between integration and suicide is neither linear as Durkheim implies in his inverse law nor U-shaped as they interpret his hypothesis. Durkheim hypothesized an inverse relationship between integration and the overall suicide rate. But when Durkheim examines highly integrated societies or groups, he focuses more on the different ways they produce suicide than on comparing their rate of suicide with poorly integrated societies or groups. He does not state that the overall rates of suicide increase in highly integrated groups—only the rate of altruistic suicides increase in highly integrated societies. In fact, the only comparisons he makes are between civilian and military suicide which are higher due to the tightly knit character of those groups. There is an implicit caveat, highly integrated groups must have norms that require or encourage suicide before they generate altruistic suicides. Thus, either a linear relation would apply to highly integrated groups with no norms requiring suicide or perhaps a U-shaped relation to those highly integrated groups who had many norms requiring suicide. This also assumes the number of altruistic suicides would increase at the same rate in comparison to the rate of egoistic suicides. Rather than a U-shaped distribution, a J-shaped distribution may better characterize the shape of the rates of altruistic suicides. Additionally, Durkheim uses the overall suicide rate to analyze the rates of altruistic suicides; however, there is no discussion of the number of norms requiring altruistic suicide or the number of individuals affected by those norms. Both of these variables would have an effect on the rates of altruistic suicide within highly integrated societies. Instead of one hypothesis characterizing the relationship between integration and suicide, two additional possibilities could exist. If all degrees of integrated societies had no norms requiring suicide, the inverse relation would hold. If some highly integrated societies had some norms requiring suicide that affected some individuals, the suicide rate would increase somewhat, manifesting a J-shaped relationship. If all highly integrated societies had many norms requiring suicide that affected many individuals, the suicide rate would increase significantly, manifesting a U-shaped relationship.

Similar problems arise with the dimension of regulation. As earlier chapters have outlined the different ways in which anomie is created, one cannot assess the impact that each of these factors have on the overall rate of regulation. This creates the problem that one cannot assess how many anomic suicides are solely due to regulating appetites in comparison to barriers of social structures or the restrictions of the larger society. Given two societies at the same level of under-regulation, their suicide rates may differ due to one society having an additional condition of structural barriers. Thus, the relation between the two independent variables and suicide are more complex than Durkheim represents in his theory. It is argued here that Merton's contribution of goal disjunction impairing opportunities is more aligned with fatalistic suicide than anomic suicide and tied to a theory of deviance rather than cohesion. Furthermore, since no real-world examples of overly restrictive norms were identified by Durkheim in fatalistic suicide, additional information has to be included on the opportunity structure in societies causing fatalistic suicide. These are presumed to be independent of the degree of restraint of appetites. This is not envisioned at all by Durkheim's original formulation.

Ambiguities in the theory

(A) Durkheim's lack of clarity in defining the independent variables resulted in diverse interpretations of the concept of "integration" in the literature: (a) common social meanings, beliefs and practices, (b) patterns of interaction or networks of social relationships, (c) a balance of egoistic and anomic forces in society, (d) organization and unity, and (e) attunement or intersubjectivity, have been associated with the concept of integration in the literature and research studies. He also did not operationally define or empirically measure integration of any group or society and thereby establish more convincingly the validity of his hypothesis.

The same is true for the concept of regulation. He did not present a clear definition of regulation, develop operational definitions or measure the degree of regulation of any group or society and consequently a variety of meanings have also evolved associated with anomie, especially in the area of social deviance. It has been referred to as normlessness or the absence of norms, the failure of the norms to regulate conduct, social disintegration, personal disintegration, conflicting norms, etc.

(B) Durkheim frequently fails to distinguish culture (a system of social meanings) from social organization or social structure (patterns of social interaction or social relationships). He links patterns of suicide to both variables interchangeably believing that he is tracing the statistical patterns of suicide to attributes of moral structures when many are linked to systems of social interaction, social structure, or social organization, and instead, he doesn't distinguish them from each other as different aspects of society. Sometimes, they are difficult to separate as they are intertwined. For example, when Durkheim investigated the role of dynamic density in the size of families relationship to suicide rates, he asserted higher dynamic density intensified the reality, potency, and continual presence of the family as a social force in people's lives, strengthening its moral structure's ability to control and unify people's lives. These intertwined forces increase integration, and yet, Durkheim fails to highlight that the frequency of social interaction influences the strength of the moral structure and subsequently affects the overall rate of integration and solely focuses on the moral structures in regards to defining integration.

(C) Durkheim also contributes to the ambiguity of his major concepts when he states "integration" refers to "feelings of solidarity," "esprit-de-corps," and "cohesiveness"—which more properly should be regarded as products or consequences of integration rather than part of the definition of integration. Durkheim fails to distinguish between (a) the nature of integration from (b) the causes of integration, and (c) its consequences. This confusion exists in his central concept of integration (Berk 2006) and extends to regulation as well.

(D) Durkheim does not specify differences in moralities and norms that make a difference in his predictions with regard to rates of suicide. First, in regard to mechanical solidarity and integration, Durkheim only focuses on the number of norms, their strength, and how extensively they cover social life which determine how tightly they bind society and people together; however, the content of the norms can be important in emphasizing group orientations over individual interests. In *The Division of Labor*, he points out whether the norms emphasize individualism or collectivism in the cult of the individual. Douglas emphasizes that some norms are orientations toward the collectivity and create more solidarity (Douglas 1967). Thus, the content of the norms are important. The emphasis on the collective versus the individual will be related to the degree of solidarity the norms create. A second way the content of the norms are important for Durkheim is whether they regulate conduct or appetites, which in anomic suicide cause a difference between Merton's and Durkheim's theories of anomie. A third way the type of norms matter is in altruistic suicide, as highly integrated groups only manifest suicide when there are norms that demand or encourage it.

(E) Durkheim does not elaborate sufficiently the role of the intervening variables in explicating the relationship between integration and suicide, nor does he show how the intervening variables can affect each other and does not explicitly state that he is not offering a singular theory of egoistic suicide, but several different hypotheses and intervening variables between integration and suicide are being proposed. Integration can, therefore, contribute to suicide in quite different ways that are not clearly identified by him.

a The lack of integration can *cause* suicidal impulses. Low integration causes feelings of meaninglessness and purposelessness in persons, and these feelings, in turn, cause suicide. Social isolation can also contribute to suicide in different ways.

Depending on which definition of integration is employed, different hypotheses can be generated.

Hypothesis 1: Groups with few shared meanings cause larger numbers of individuals with suicidal impulses. (i) Those most divergent from the shared meanings are most likely to take their lives.
Hypothesis 2: Groups with few social relationships cause large numbers of suicides. (i) Those most isolated will be the ones to take their lives.

b Group integration can *aggravate* already existing suicidal impulses. Here impulses result from life's misfortunes but are intensified by the individual's excessive self-concern from a lack of integration or from the lack of supportive social relationships.

Hypothesis 1: Groups with few shared meanings intensify people's misfortunes which creates more suicides.
Hypothesis 2: Groups with few social relations intensify misfortunes and cause increased suicides.

This presumes that the number of misfortunes is constant or that their effect is insufficient to cause suicide, and the degree of amplification is what intensifies them to be sufficient to cause suicide. No individual predictions can be made since there is no way to predict individual misfortunes.

c Group integration can *restrain* suicidal impulses.

Thus, the linkages in the theory are not clearly spelled out. Are feelings of meaninglessness sufficient by themselves to cause the individual to take their life? Or, do they merely serve to make the individual more vulnerable to life's misfortunes, which are the main precipitating factor of suicide? The role of society is not clearly spelled out or explicated in his analysis. It can *cause suicidal impulses to develop in the individual, amplify already existing suicidal impulses, or restrain already existing suicidal impulses; however, all or any combination of these could contribute to the overall suicide rate.* Precisely how integration works and its effects are not clearly elucidated in the main body of the theory.

Contradictions in Durkheim's theory

(A) Durkheim's inverse law of degrees of integration and suicide rates is contradicted by his investigation of altruistic suicide. (a) He found a highly integrated group, the army, had higher rates of suicide than the less integrated civilian sector, and (b) that the rate of suicide in highly integrated societies is a function of the number of norms requiring or encouraging suicide and is not determined by the degree of integration in the society. A highly integrated society with norms prohibiting suicide would have low rates and with many norms requiring suicide would have high rates. Therefore, these facts do not conform and may contradict the law of inverse relations.

Durkheim's investigation of altruistic suicide also differed significantly from his analysis of egoistic suicide where he primarily explored differences in *rates of suicide* among groups with differing degrees of integration to establish that integration was the key factor causing suicide. In contrast, when exploring altruistic suicide, he focused very little on comparing rates of suicide of highly integrated with less integrated groups. Instead, he focused primarily on the differences in how highly integrated societies caused suicide than less well integrated groups. In altruistic societies, it was the presence of society, and particularly its moral prescriptions, which caused suicides, and he identified the different forms, processes, and ways suicides were brought about by society. His supportive evidence relied largely upon examples from different societies.

An exception was his comparison of suicides in the army, a highly integrated group, with the civilian population, a less integrated group. He found the rates higher among soldiers than civil society. Not only were suicide rates higher in the military than the civilian population but were higher the longer a person was in the army, and among officers and volunteers, all of which are indicative of high degrees of integration within the military. However, his example of military suicides contradicts his inverse law. It is only one case and not of a total society but a group within society, so it is hard to come to a definitive conclusion about highly integrated societies. The analysis suggests social environments like societies are more complex and cannot be characterized by a single designation as loosely integrated.

Durkheim was perhaps deliberately ambiguous about whether he was attempting to account for the frequency of suicides in highly integrated societies. The reason for this is that it complicates synthesizing his theory and describing the overall relationship between integration and suicide across the total spectrum of integration in linear terms. Closer examination reveals that it is not possible to predict the frequency of suicides in highly integrated societies from knowledge of its degree of integration alone. The volume of suicides of tightly knit or highly integrated societies depends on the content of the norms, the number that require or encourage suicide, and power to control conduct. In highly integrated societies, the only certainty is that people are more likely to conform to whatever norms exist. If there are many norms making suicide obligatory, optional or encouraged, then suicide rates will be high in those altruistic societies. Conversely, when the norms only prohibit suicide, then the rates will be extremely low in those altruistic societies.

Durkheim may have limited the scope of his inverse law to only societies or groups on the egoistic spectrum of integration, but never explicitly stated that limitation. Most scholars construe the law to apply over the total range of integrated societies—to which it does not appear to apply.

In any case, the overall relationship between integration and suicide rates depends on the content, power, and number of norms in highly integrated societies—which clashes with Durkheim's law of inverse relationships. According to Durkheim, altruistic suicide is caused by the moral system and what it dictates, *not by tightly knit bonds or strong cohesive forces*, as these conditions only increase the likelihood people will obey those moral prescriptions. Therefore, only highly integrated societies that require or encourage self-sacrifice have high rates of suicide. Highly integrated societies that condemn or do not require suicide will have low rates. Integration is not sufficient to predict rates of suicide for highly integrated societies.

Therefore, *the relationship between integration and suicide cannot be inverse or even linear or curvilinear, as Durkheim hypothesized earlier*, due to fact that it is not the degree of integration that is solely responsible for suicide rates. It is, in highly integrated societies, a function of what the morals require, that is critical in influencing the rates of suicide in each altruistic society. In addition, suicides in those societies do not result from the lack of attachment to society but from attachment to systems whose norms require self-sacrifice. This conclusion casts doubts on the many studies using multiple regression analyses to analyze the data whose assumptions are not met by Durkheim's theory.

(B) Although Durkheim never explicitly enunciated the U-shaped relationship between integration and regulation and suicide rates, a linear or curvilinear relationship between integration and suicide is also inconsistent with Durkheim's analysis of altruistic suicide since the suicide rates of highly integrated societies depend on the content of the moral prescriptions not on integration.

(C) Similar problems arise when applying either a linear or U-shaped relationship between regulation and suicide rates. Closer analysis reveals that regulation by itself also is not sufficient to predict suicide rates since the satisfaction of social appetites that attaches people to society does not just depend on regulating their appetites. It also depends upon the opportunities to satisfy those appetites that exist in the individual's social circumstances. According to Merton's influential interpretation of Durkheim's concept of anomie (1938), anomie is caused by the degree of disjunction between cultural goals and the socially acceptable avenues for achieving the goals and the social structure limiting access to those goals. Class structures or patterns of racial discrimination are examples of structural barriers. Thus, Durkheim unwittingly involved social structures in determining anomie and anomic pressures by limiting the means available to achieve the desired social goals. Merton (1968) recognized social strain resulting from the disjunction between culturally desired goals and socially structured means create anomic pressures causing many forms of deviance in addition to suicide. He applies Durkheim's postulate that "suicide is a normal response to abnormal social pressures" to all forms of deviance showing deviance is not alien to society, a central plank of sociological perspectives of most forms of social deviance. Therefore, to predict whether people's appetites will be sufficiently satisfied requires knowledge of the role social structure plays in limiting access to those goals in those social contexts. Measures of regulation alone will be insufficient to predict suicide rates. Thus, restraints must be judged in terms of what the environment provides, which may be reflected in Durkheim's notion that poverty is a restraint—expectations become lowered with the experience of continual deprivation. This additional information is required but is not included in the U-shaped hypothesis. If the social structure impairs goal attainment, it vitiates the effects of regulation; or, if society does not produce goals or make them attainable, for whatever reason, it will alter the impact of regulation since appetites could not be satisfied by society in either case. The hypothesis about the degree of regulation could not be confirmed since the goals would not be available irrespective of the degree of regulation.

A more radical reading of Durkheim's theory of anomie as a critique of capitalism is that it gives rise to limitless appetites, greed and self-interest that weaken social solidarity as well as casting individuals toward the abyss. Since the source of the problem is capitalism, the system itself and can't be restrained by government, it must be replaced with socialism as an alternative to enhancing solidarity and improving the quality of life. His critique of capitalism would be that it attenuates ties in the moral community and casts people into continual frustration, despair, and suicide. The critical variable with respect to regulation is the pervasiveness of capitalism in the society.

Therefore, the current consensus view of a "U" shaped relationship between both integration and regulation does not accurately represent the relationships as they are described throughout all aspects of the text, and also these proposed relationships would not be true in the synthesis of Durkheim's theory. Integration is also not the proximate cause of altruistic suicide, and highly integrated societies have a wide range of suicide rates; therefore, the relationship is not linear. Secondly, regulation, by itself, is insufficient to predict suicide rates without considering aspects of the social structure, so the relationship also cannot be linear or curvilinear. The assumed synthesis does not fit the theory very well when these aspects are considered. In addition, scholars who saw a departure in the later part of *Suicide* from its early parts also fail to note the contradictions and incomplete specification of the theory and offered no other way to synthesize the theory. *In any case, the theory is incomplete as it stands.*

Those who claim integration and regulation are indistinguishable might describe anomie as a result of the lack of unity or of the parts of society working in concert or fitting together. Another way is to define regulation in terms of the degree of conflict or balance between goals and acceptable avenues for obtaining them and the society's social structure and abundance or scarcity of cultural goals.

(D) Another contradiction or inconsistency in Durkheim's analysis of suicide is with respect to the evidence in his tracing the origins of integration and regulation. Durkheim believes the moral structure of society gives rise to both forces.

Origin of Integration: In the *DLS* (1893), he cited the diminishing collective conscience as critical to weakening the social bonds attaching individuals to society. In *Suicide* (1897), while exploring egoistic suicide, and viewing the suicide rate as an index of weakened social bonds, Durkheim argued that differences in suicide rates of religious, family and political groups were related to differences in their moral structure's ability to control the conduct of group members. Another link he found early in his study examining society's aptitude for suicide was between industrialization and increasing suicide rates. In the *DLS* (1893), he asserted industrialization diminished the collective conscience or moral structure. And in *Suicide*, he traced altruistic suicide directly to specific norms in the moral structure demanding or encouraging self-sacrifice. Highly integrated societies, however, had a robust and powerful moral structure that impelled individuals to take their lives. Thus, he traced three links between the moral structure and suicide rates supporting his belief that the social force of integration emanated from the moral structure of society.

However, Durkheim linked the origin of several other of the statistical patterns of suicide to social interaction, finding that it varied during the course of a day and over the year causing similar variations in suicide rates. He also linked the lower suicide rates of large families to variations in dynamic density, also an aspect of social interaction. He linked other variations like the difference between sexes to differences in their social roles, and related variations in suicide rates to social organization like industrialization and others to group membership. Thus, many of the origins of the social forces were linked to aspects of social structure and not the moral structure of society, contradicting a main conclusion of his study.

Durkheim did not consistently make a distinction between the social structure (patterns of interaction) and the moral structure (cultural patterns of acts, ideas, and sentiments based on symbols). Often times, it is difficult to differentiate them in reality as they are so intertwined. Durkheim viewed social interaction as an important augmenting factor in the power of moral beliefs in his analysis of dynamic density in the role of family size and suicide, a theme he developed in his theory of rituals in his investigation of religion (1912). In many cases, however, the differences between culture and social structure are clear and significant. The Social Network Analysis's interpretation of Durkheim's theory looking at the overall structure of social relationships make different predictions than those who adopt the "moral structural" interpretation of integration. The differences and contradictions are clear when Durkheim discuses society's role in intensifying misfortunes. He points to supportive social relationships buffering the shocks of misfortunes which clearly ties his analysis to the social structure not the moral structure of society. Pescosolido and Georgiana (1989) argue in the relation between church attendance and suicide that church attendance or interaction intensifies the moral beliefs. Closer examination is needed to see if it is sharing the beliefs or the social relationship itself which offers the protection against suicide to test Durkheim's theory.[10]

Thus, some of his examples challenge his conclusion that the moral structure is the uniting factor in society. Sometimes the moral and social structure of society are so inter-related they cannot be separated. At other times, they clearly have distinctive manifestations, and both the moral and social structures give rise to the social forces. The least that can be said is that both the moral and social structures give rise to integration and make room for Social Network Analysis under Durkheim's theory.

Origin of Regulation: Durkheim's efforts to trace the origin of regulation to the moral structure are not as clear or well-focused as those linking integration to the moral structure. For example, he does not explicitly connect the shrinking of the collective conscience during industrialization to deregulation of desires in either *DLS* or *Suicide*. He introduced the concept of anomie in the *DLS* as a consequence of rapid social change during industrialization where a temporary lack of guidance by the moral structure developed until new morals emerged and more tenuously to pathologies in the *Division of Labor*. However, in that analysis, anomie was *more related to integration than to regulation as he makes no specific reference to the lack of regulation of aspirations during that period of rapid change, just the absence of norms.* He ties the lack of guidance by norms during rapid change to readjustment in the social hierarchy. Another condition he relates to anomic suicide is the rise of materialism caused by industrialization and an accompanying rise of capitalism, which alters values and aspirations in the moral structure by heightening expectations unrealistically, leading to frustration and fueling suicides. A fourth condition Durkheim links to anomic suicide, enunciated in *Suicide*, is to fluctuations in economic conditions that are related to changes in suicide rates. They create serious dislocations in society, and for Durkheim, are evidence of moral crises. They impact people's desires and society's ability to satisfy those desires, impairing regulation causing anomic suicides. He presents little evidence to support that economic fluctuations are primarily moral crises, and these crises cause suicides.

In investigating regulation, Durkheim focuses only on those changes in the moral structure that relate to shaping people's expectations about what is realistic to expect from life in their positions in society. A serious *problem in his analysis is that many of the changes in the moral structure could be viewed as impacting integration more than regulation and goes to the question of how separate integration and regulation are.*

Economic changes are not only associated with changing suicide rates but many other forms of non-conformity such as murder, crime, addiction, mental illness, etc. These economic changes are reflective of a general breakdown of society's ability to control all behavior, linking them to integration more than regulation.

Durkheim also argues industrialization enriches societies and emphasizes materialism, creating new desires often intensified by the emergence of consumer capitalism giving rise to unbridled greed, unrealistic expectations and self-interest altering moral beliefs in society and impacting the moral structure.

A key factor to satisfaction of appetites not explicitly recognized by materialism, is the opportunities provided by society which may have to be included in fully understanding whether there is sufficient appetite gratification by society, in addition to just the regulation of aspirations.

Some aspects of satisfaction are related to the moral structure's ability to regulate desires and other aspects of satisfaction are related to the opportunities available in the social context. Merton's (1968) interpretation of Durkheim's theory of anomie focused on the degree of disjunction between the cultural goals and the social structure's ability to provide sufficient avenues for members to attain those goals. The more the social structure acts as a barrier limiting opportunities for some to attain those goals, the more disjunction exists which creates anomic pressures. The greater the goal disjunction the stronger the anomic forces and greater rate of non-conforming behavior, or suicide in the focus of this study. Merton broadened the theory of anomie to include all forms of deviance asserting Durkheim's insight that "deviance is a normal response to abnormal social pressures." Merton focused on the unfairness of specific systems which fall most heavily on certain sectors of the population. Thus, Durkheim unwittingly included the social structure as part of the process inducing anomic pressures. However, it might be argued Durkheim included this consideration into the concept of appropriate regulation which is factored in when you determine what is likely possible in each social context.

Merton's (1968) interpretation of Durkheim's theory gives it a new twist focusing on the role of the social structures, like class or race, in creating anomic pressures, rather than focusing on the moral structure. He also identifies populations most subject to anomic pressures. The origin of anomic pressures is the result of a disjunction between the moral and social structure where the social structure limits opportunities to achieve social goals for some members of society. Thus, it is social barriers rather than aspects of the moral structure which causes anomic pressures which Durkheim doesn't discuss specifically.

Another cause of deregulation and anomic pressures which Durkheim ascribed to a property of the moral system takes place during periods of rapid change when new norms have not yet arisen to regulate aspirations, and in the moral void, anomic pressures arise. Durkheim does not elaborate how they specifically impact aspirations. In fatalistic suicide and some of the examples Durkheim cites, it is not just the moral structure that creates the pressure, but society's inability to provide access to the social goals that gives rise to those pressures, although they are not discussed by Durkheim.

Durkheim, in developing the concept of regulation, *involved aspects of the social structure giving rise to the social forces causing suicide. This challenges his belief that the forces emanated solely from the moral structure—a grave oversight.* It challenges his belief that the forces causing suicide emanated completely from the moral structure of society. His formulation of anomie and fatalistic suicide and the examples he uses to illustrate them, were also linked to the social structure, or at least, it has been interpreted in this manner by Merton (1968). His article "Social Structure and Anomie" enunciates this interpretation clearly and has been accepted by many others. The reason for the divergences between Durkheim's and Merton's conceptions of anomie is that Merton's is a theory of social order, an aspect of integration, and Durkheim's a theory of social solidarity, an aspect of regulation.

It can be concluded from these facts that at minimum Durkheim has to acknowledge that both the moral and social structures give rise to both the forces of integration and regulation.

Notes

1 This principle is developed more fully in Durkheim's (1912) exploration of the unifying role of religion as the glue holding society together and the importance of ritual in unifying the group as people come together affirming the importance and unity of the group. Rituals make the individual feel a part of a larger whole and not only unify the group but create emotional effervescence supercharging society's power over individuals with an added sense of awe and animation. These rituals need to be repeated to keep the existence of the group alive in people's minds. This emphasizes the inextricability of social interaction from the power of culture.

2 Turner also identifies social interaction as a factor creating social cohesion (1990:1097). Breault asserts "Durkheim plainly means the degree to which people are attached, bonded, or connected to each other. Durkheim is talking about social and emotional ties and the amount of intensity of such bonds" (1994:13). But Durkheim refers to the degree of social control creating bonds to the group much more frequently than to social relationships.

3 Pope asserts Durkheim also fails to distinguish belief from actions (1976:15). See also Bellah (1959:460).

4 A way of reconciling the different perspectives of integration is to recognize the numerous ways societies have of exercising control over people's behavior. One

is through instilling norms into individuals, a second is by close surveillance by others, peer pressure, and informal sanctions, a third is external formal social controls and sanctions, a fourth is through social constructions like the collective conscience or fictions that govern peoples' beliefs and behavior, and others.

5 Turner proposed a similar notion: "The total suicide rate of the society is a result of the equilibrium-producing composition that occurs between 'opposed' forces that produce suicide" (1986:139).

6 Stedman Jones gives more emphasis to Douglas's work and on a balance in the moral system than most scholars (2013:165–166)

7 A fourth type, "functional" integration, referred to mutual dependence resulting from specialization in the division of labor. Durkheim's analysis of egoistic suicide was based on mechanical solidarity, cohesion resulting from shared values, norms, and beliefs (i.e., shared culture) and not organic solidarity.

8 Durkheim, discussing small families, states that feelings for each other may be more important than the moral structure in the bonds that unite them, so emotions can play an important role in social bonds (1952:160).

9 Though he continued searching for effective mechanisms of integrating modern society after *Suicide* (1897).

10 Durkheim's work gave impetus to the field of sociology of illness which assumes people's physical and psychological well-being are related to the richness of their social networks.

6

RESOLVING THE AMBIGUITIES AND CONTRADICTIONS IN DURKHEIM'S THEORY

Greater specificity is needed in both identifying the objectives and accomplishments of Durkheim's study and resolving the ambiguities and contradictions in his theory

(A) One ambiguity in *Suicide* is whether Durkheim's theory either attempts to or actually accounts for the volume of suicides found in each society. In *Suicide*, Durkheim concludes that "at each moment of its history, therefore, *each society has a definite aptitude for suicide* (1952:xlv)." Durkheim cites statistical regularities that support this conclusion showing each society produces its own characteristic volume of suicides every year, almost as though it has a quota of suicides. Each society has a collective inclination for suicide that afflicts it, and Durkheim argues it takes a year to complete the annual cycle of social activities to fulfill the quota. Durkheim's theory asserts the strength of the social forces each society produces determines the volume and forms of suicide in that society. In *Suicide* (1897), after he investigates the evidence that suicide is socially caused, he leaves the impression that his study will account for the volume of suicides with which each society is afflicted. Yet, closer examination reveals that the theory cannot account for the volume of suicides each society manifests since he lacks any measurements of the independent variables. Nowhere in the study does Durkheim show the ability of his theory to account for those facts.

One reason the theory lacks that ability is that Durkheim failed to develop measures of the degree of integration or regulation of each society or group he examined so that a quantitative assessment of the strength of the independent variable could be assessed and related to specific volumes of suicides in each society.

DOI: 10.4324/9781003669272-6

(B) *The study does not fully establish that the moral structure is the sole or primary source of integration and regulation.* It is unclear whether Durkheim's evidence was sufficient to establish that it was the moral structure of society that gave rise to the social forces that determined its inclination toward suicide, or was it the power of his rhetoric that was so convincing to readers? The evidence he presents in support of the proposition "the moral structure generates the social currents of egoism, altruism and anomie[1] that run through society acting as forces on individuals causing them to take their lives" is inconclusive. Durkheim never convincingly establishes that the sole or primary cause of societal quotas or inclinations toward suicide is society's moral structure. The closest he comes to supporting this proposition is his investigation of the role integration plays in producing the differences in suicide rates between religious groups. He argued earlier in the *DLS* (1893) that a major consequence of specialization of the division of labor during industrialization was the diminishing of the collective conscience and the decline of mechanical solidarity weakening bonds in modern society. In *Suicide*, he traces one consequence of weakened social bonds to increasing suicide rates in society. He argued that the differences in suicide rates between religious groups can be accounted for by the degree of integration or shared beliefs and values of the group. The degree to which the religion permits or encourages "free inquiry" is a negative index of integration. Therefore, Catholics, because they have more common beliefs than Protestants, religions with centralized authority structures which serve to render tradition invariable, and who are minorities in their country which unify them, are more integrated which explains why they have lower suicide rates. This evidence supports his hypothesis that the moral system of values and beliefs and the forces of mechanical solidarity produce integration that bond individuals to one another and their groups. These analyses, however, fail to control for even economic differences between the groups.

Since Durkheim lacked any empirical measurements of the degree of integration of the religious group, it is not possible to assess either how much group members actually agree on their beliefs, one aspect of integration, or how much they conform to those beliefs to assess the extent of social control, another aspect of integration, each religious group exercised over their members. The evidence in support of the hypothesis is not strong. Absent of such quantitative assessments, no predictions can be made with respect to the volume or rate each society or group would manifest. A rank order correlation between integration and suicide rates could reveal the nature and strength of the relationship between the variables but could not lead to predictions about the actual volume of suicide with which each group was afflicted, especially since there are four different forces that contribute to the total volume of suicides. The variables also may not have a linear or curvilinear relationship to the suicide rates requiring modern multi-variance analyses. Therefore, no conclusion can be reached with regard to what objectives could realistically be pursued in his study with these limitations.

He offers other supporting evidence for his hypothesis by examining differences between those individuals who belong to groups, such as the married, those belonging to larger families, and those experiencing unifying crises which show a pattern of results that support his conclusion but are not rigorous proofs. Again, it is hard to differentiate if the group authority and shared morality or social relationships are most important in affecting the suicide rate. His assertion that it takes a whole year for the quota of suicides to be fulfilled suggests social interaction drives the process generating suicide.

Durkheim contradicts his conclusion that it is solely the moral structure that gives rise to the force of integration when he links variations in suicide rates to patterns of social interaction, social organization, social structure, and social roles sprinkled throughout his treatise which suggests that both the social structure and the moral structure give rise to the suicidal forces of integration in society.

Durkheim is even less explicit tracing the origins of regulation than he was in tracing the links of integration to the moral system. He detected the presence of anomic forces from observing fluctuations in suicide rates during business cycles. He begins his investigation with the conclusion that what these cycles constitute, at their core, are moral crises. This is because economic downturns don't just make people poorer, but they result in the declassification of individual's moral rankings in society. Because if the main effect of economic contractions is to increase poverty, poverty is a protection against suicide as the poor have low rates of suicide. Therefore, suicide rates should decrease in economic downturns, but instead, they increase. He concludes that what explains this increase in suicides is that they are moral crises but presents no further evidence to support his conclusion.

Losing or gaining ground with respect to others is disorienting, attenuating individual's ties to their moral guidelines impacting their aspirations, goals, and assessment of their lot in life and progress toward their goals, and these effects are related to issues of regulation and conditions leading to anomie described by Durkheim.

However, economic expansions should be equally disorienting and increase suicide rates as they are also moral crises, but they do not, challenging Durkheim's conclusions. Anecdotally, vast increases in wealth over short periods by lottery winners or dot-com billionaires have shown some disorientation and psychological problems which support his analysis, but few if any suicides have been noted.

Durkheim's primary argument tracing deregulation to moral structures is found in his discussion of the emergence of materialism and consumer capitalism in modern society that gives rise to anomie. He points out that individuals in these societies are exposed to moral values such as acquisitiveness and self-interest and that these societies fail to regulate or limit those appetites. Lacking any guidelines or regulation, individuals develop an infinity of desires and insatiable greed. This results in feelings that they never have enough, and they continually focus on what they lack instead of what they have. This results in perpetual dissatisfaction and frustration in their inability to satisfy their limitless desires which creates unbearable frustration culminating in suicide.

Thus, it is the failure of the moral system to regulate or limit appetites which causes individuals to feel that society does not provide sufficient satisfaction to make life worthwhile. This results in a failure to attach individuals sufficiently to society, weakening the hold of its norms and subsequently creating anomie and fragmenting social bonds.

The evidence he relies upon is that richer societies have higher suicide rates than poorer societies, and richer individuals and those with occupations more closely tied to finance have higher suicide rates than poorer individuals and those with occupations unrelated to finance.

This reasoning breaks down, however, when Durkheim traces the origin of over-regulation and fatalistic suicide. In the little space he devotes to fatalistic suicide, he ties excessive regulation and fatalism to the organization of society and social structure rather than to moral systems. Fatalistic suicide does not result from the frustrations of insatiable appetites but from situations where individuals cannot obtain satisfaction of their appetites because of the way society is organized. Slaves in pre-modern societies or inmates in prison in modern societies are often cited as examples since Durkheim does not develop this aspect of his theory. They also cannot obtain satisfaction of their appetites because of the structures of slavery and prison that stand in their way of obtaining the level of satisfaction of their desires that makes life tolerable.

Therefore, like integration, Durkheim also links regulation to aspects of social structure without explicitly acknowledging it. Merton's (1968) article, "Social Structure and Anomie," is the most influential interpretation of Durkheim's theory of anomie. Yet, Merton gives primacy to the social structure's role in creating anomie and seems to depart from Durkheim's emphasis on the lack of regulation by the moral system of society.

Merton defines anomie as a breakdown of the norm's ability to regulate conduct and agrees somewhat with Durkheim's description as an absence of rules, but Durkheim focuses more on deregulation of aspirations or appetites than on conduct. They differ with respect to the causes of anomie. Durkheim attributes the causes of anomie to the failure of the moral system to limit individual's appetites, and Merton attributes the causes of anomie to the social structure obstructing certain segments of society from obtaining cultural goals.

Merton asserts anomie results from the social structure, such as class, race, gender, or other hierarchies and patterns of discrimination, obstructing or limiting segments of the population's ability to obtain cultural goals. Thus, what Durkheim describes as a "lack of regulation problem," Merton sees as a "fairness of opportunity" problem.

They also differ in exploring the consequences of anomie. Whereas Durkheim focuses solely on suicide, Merton explores a range of responses or deviant patterns of adaptation to anomie. Merton employs Durkheim's hypotheses stating the stronger the anomic forces, the higher the rate of deviance (suicide), and those individuals exposed to those social forces are those likely to engage in deviance (commit suicide). Deviance is a normal response to abnormal social pressures. Merton ties the strength of the social forces to the severity of the impediment of the social structure. Durkheim, outside economic fluctuations, does not develop much about what influences the increases or decreases in regulation in society.

To resolve these problems in his theory, a more precise specification is needed of the linkage of the intervening variables between (a) the moral systems role and the social structures role in generating the social forces of both integration and regulation and (b) the linkages or intervening variables between extremes in integration and regulation showing how they produce suicides. In addition, measurements of the independent variables of integration and regulation are needed to determine the percentage of variance each variable explains as well as the volume of suicides with which each society is afflicted. More effort must be directed toward differentiating moral systems (culture) from social structure (patterns of interaction). Furthermore, the problems of identifying and measuring attachment to society and distinguishing this from interpersonal bonds or social connections are also complex but will add clarity and resolve some ambiguities in helping clarify Durkheim's theory.

(C) Both interpretations of Durkheim's theory, the traditional and the consensus view, cannot be supported by a close reading of Durkheim's analyses of how each variable produces suicide. First, there is a contradiction between his "inverse law" and the traditional and consensus interpretations of his theory. His analysis of altruistic suicide also contradicts the inverse law and the traditional and consensus views of his theory. He found, for example, in his analysis of altruistic suicide, the more integrated group, the army, had higher suicide rates than the less integrated civilian sector of society, which seemingly contradicts the inverse law. One way to reconcile the contradiction was to argue his inverse law was limited to groups and societies on the weakly integrated spectrum of the continuum rather than to all groups on the spectrum of integration. The consensus view emerged as a more elegant way of reconciling the apparent contradiction by postulating the U-shaped relation between integration and suicide rates arguing both extremes of the continuum manifest high rates, and then this principle could also be applied to the relationship between regulation and suicide rates.

However, assuming highly integrated groups necessarily had high suicide rates does not follow Durkheim's analysis of altruistic suicide or conform to the facts. His chapter on altruistic suicide focused primarily on the differences by which high and low levels of integration brought about suicide not on the volume of suicides of highly integrated groups. He did present data on the military and compared them with civilian suicides but largely to show how the military's culture was a key factor in causing suicide.

A deeper examination of his analysis of the etiology of altruistic suicide challenges both the inverse law, the traditional interpretation of a linear, and the consensus view of a U-shaped relation between integration and suicide rates. Because what is responsible for altruistic suicides are social norms that encourage or require suicide. Highly integrated groups that lack such norms will not produce suicides. Strong integration only increases the likelihood they will obey those norms should they exist in society. What determines the rate of suicide in highly integrated societies are the number of such norms, their strength, and number of individuals subject to them. Durkheim does not incorporate this understanding into his theory or hypotheses and, therefore, the relationship between suicide and integration could not be predicted as either inverse, linear, or U-shaped, because the relevant variables, information about the norms, are not included in the theory. Thus, neither the consensus nor traditional view of Durkheim's theory is supported by Durkheim's own analysis. Both information about the existence of norms requiring suicide and the degree of integration of the group are required to make predictions of the suicide rate. Durkheim fails to recognize or incorporate these considerations in his hypotheses. Or if he did, this may be the reason he never presented an overall summary of the theory showing how all the pieces of the theory fit together. The content, strength, and number of individuals subject to the norms are the key to the volume of suicides in highly integrated societies.

Therefore, with these facts missing, no relationships, linear or U-shaped, can be predicted until the relevant variables are incorporated into the theory, as it stands incomplete currently.

The postulated relation between regulation and suicide rates in Durkheim's theory may be equally problematic and inadequately characterized by either the traditional or consensus view. The problem is similar to integration in that variables influencing the relation between regulation and suicide are not included in Durkheim's hypotheses.

The consensus view asserts Durkheim hypothesized under and over regulation of appetites produce social forces causing high rates of anomic and fatalistic suicides, respectively.

Without restraint, an individual's appetites become insatiable, and with excessive restraint, they are thwarted at every turn. Both conditions cause unbearable frustration due to the lack of sufficient satisfaction to make life worthwhile and ultimately lead to suicide. As these appetites have a social origin, only society can exercise the necessary restraint to keep them moderated.

However, more clarity is needed as to exactly what aspects of society restrain individual's appetites. Durkheim implicates the moral system as key in failing to regulate appetites. Materialism and capitalism give rise to moral values that foster unlimited desires and insatiable greed and, therefore, fail to limit the individual's horizons. However, Durkheim also states the experience of poverty teaches restraint. Therefore, those on the bottom of capitalist societies are exposed to different forces and restraints as those in the upper reaches of society. Durkheim, thus, indirectly introduces the social structure as a form of restraint in society but does not include it explicitly in his theory or hypotheses in the same fashion he ignored the normative system of highly integrated societies as a key factor causing suicide.

Merton's (1968) article interprets Durkheim's theory differently than either the traditional or consensus view of Durkheim's theory. Merton cites social structural barriers as the key element causing anomie rather than limitless desires. The continual frustration individuals experience attempting to achieve the culturally induced goals due to obstruction by the social structure weakens the hold the norms have on individuals creating deregulation or anomie. Thus, for Merton, anomie is caused by the social structures limiting access to goals for certain segments of society, and not on continually escalating desires. He also limits anomic forces to those experiencing the blocked avenues to goal attainment.

For Merton, anomie can be eliminated when the goal disjunction is corrected, but he does not make it clear if this requires only making access more equal by creating a level playing field or that society must provide a certain level of goal attainment in the population. In either case, it is not capitalism that creates the problem but discriminatory patterns within society that create anomie. Durkheim's assessment is a more radical critique by postulating that the problems are endemic to capitalism and materialism, and they must be replaced with a system which balances self-interest with concern for society and the common good.

Merton is unclear whether unfair restraint or levels of deprivation cause anomie, but whichever is the case, he departs from Durkheim in numerous other ways as well. His version of the causes of anomie has more in common with fatalistic rather than anomic suicide because it emphasizes society's role in depriving people of fulfilling their appetites.

Merton and Durkheim also focused on different problems. Durkheim was focusing on the problem of social cohesion and one consequence of the lack of cohesion, suicide. Therefore, his investigation was drawn toward the problems of the upper reaches of society who have less restraint because of their positions in the social structure and are more prone to suicide reacting to their circumstances in society. Merton focused on the problem of social order and all forms of non-conformity directing his attention largely to how those below the upper reaches of society may suffer from more restraints. They have different experiences with either unfairness or too much restraint by the social structure and react most commonly with other forms of non-conformity than suicide, like crime, alcoholism, and addiction.

Merton introduces other ways the social structure restrains aspirations. Each person's position or role in society shapes what a person in their station can expect. Individuals also tend to compare themselves with others in their "reference groups" that also shape and temper their expectations and desires. They evaluate how well they are doing by comparing themselves with others in their reference groups, and feelings of satisfaction arise in terms of their "relative" instead of their absolute deprivation.

Merton examines alternative responses to the frustration from the social structure's obstruction and how individuals' position in social structures influences both the problems they face and their responses to pressures. Henry and Short (1954) identify people's position in the social structure as a constraint and the "strength of the relational system" determines its strength and shapes how people direct their anger and frustration and who they blame when frustrated, inward as suicide or outward as homicide.

Economic expansions impact the poor more, creating feelings that everyone is moving up and they are being left behind and blame others for their plight culminating in homicides. Economic downturns affect the rich more resulting in feelings they are losing all they have. Because the strength of their social restraints is low, they blame themselves and turn their frustration inward and commit suicide. Suicide is self-directed homicide. The social structure, therefore, plays a key role in creating problems for various segments of society and shapes individuals' responses to those problems.

Further evidence of the importance of the social structure's role in restraint in excessive regulation can be found in Durkheim's analysis of fatalistic suicides. In pre-modern societies, fatalistic suicides mostly occur as a result of the social structure limiting most opportunities for the gratification of desires. And in modern society, there are increasing parallels to the conditions Durkheim described in earlier societies.

In pre-modern India, hundreds of farmers lacking government supports or insurance during crop failures are constrained by the structure of Indian society. In modern society, it is the social structure of prison which is the instrument of oppression. In both cases, constraint is a function of aspects of social structure not moral structures of society.

From these examples, we can see Durkheim implicated the social structure in providing restraint on aspirations in several ways that are not factored in to either the traditional or consensus interpretation that make it possible to predict suicide rates due to relevant variables omitted from both formulations. Therefore, neither a linear nor a U-shaped relation can be postulated from a close reading of Durkheim's treatise.

Durkheim also did not give consideration to society's ability to satisfy appetites as a factor causing anomie or suicide. He also does not identify the intervening variables between the moral structure and regulatory forces or between the breakdown of norms and suicide or present supporting evidence. They would be helpful to resolve the ambiguity in the role of the social structure in anomic and fatalistic suicide or exactly how poverty became a restraint on aspirations and why social structural barriers do not have the same effect in a Mertonian analysis. Does the unfairness of class, gender, or ethnic barriers alter the nature of social restraint? He only indirectly ties regulation to the moral structure through disruptions or economic crises. However, he does support his conclusions with evidence, recognize the connection of regulation to the social structure, and link rates of suicide to specific aspects of the moral structure, but he does not develop overall measurements of complex societies with respect to integration or regulation, much less relate them to suicide rates. It is an exponentially more complicated problem to obtain such measures on complex societies than it would be to obtain measures on a group within society. Because he lacks measures of his independent variables, he can never establish the strength of these currents that determine the volume of suicides or the relative contribution of the various types of suicide to the overall rate in society. All he could establish is that one group has a higher rate of suicide than another. Even then, he failed to exercise all the necessary controls.

It is clear Durkheim failed to include the role of the social structure in restraining individuals' aspirations in his exploration of anomie, omitting factors that needed to be taken into account in investigating the relation between regulation and suicide rates.

(D) *It is difficult to establish how much of the variance in suicide rates Durkheim's theory can explain*: Durkheim viewed suicide rates as a composite of idiosyncratic and social suicides. But when groups were compared, it was not possible to separate the idiosyncratic from social suicides, and he assumed the idiosyncratic suicides in each group would cancel each other out, and social causes would be reflected in their differences. This made it impossible to determine what portion of the overall suicide rate was attributable to social causes. He assumed the differences in rates between the groups reflected minimal difference in social forces, but it was not possible to determine how many of the rest of the suicides were the result of social forces. Therefore, for these reasons and that no objective measurements of the independent variables, integration and regulation, were undertaken, it is not possible to assess how much of the variance his theory accounts for in the suicide rates. In other parts of his work, he argues all suicides were a consequence of the social forces including so-called idiosyncratic suicides. This question remains unresolved in analysis of Durkheim's theory. Scheff (2011) has estimated his theory accounts for under 10%, but for the stated reasons, this is not an accurate estimate. No assessment can be made as to the power of Durkheim's theory to account for the volume and patterns of suicide. The magnitude of differences in rates between groups might give some clue of the differences in strength of the various forces.

Since the relationships between integration, regulation, and suicide could be claimed to be linear or curvilinear, most commonly used statistical tools by scholars are not applicable. Thus, the theory has no way of predicting the expected volume of suicides each year based on the strength of the social forces or to show they fluctuated with the strength of the forces. In addition, because only data on the overall rate of suicide was available, he had no way to determine the relative contribution of each type of suicide to the total number of suicides. Further complicating matters is that he asserted that many suicides were blends of the various forces as well, and assessing the overall strength of individual social forces in complicatedly organized societies is already daunting at best. Differently situated groups in society contribute differently to the overall strength of forces, and the forces may have synergistic effects or even cancel each other out, making the matter quite difficult in assessing forces in any particular society and research project. Further complicating the issues is most studies rely on official statistics of suicide that do not differentiate between social causes and specific types of suicide.

(E) Durkheim's theory accounts for only a small percentage of the variances in suicide rates. Durkheim explored in even more depth the relationships between role or position in society and suicide rates and linked the differences in rates more directly to social structure when he explored gender differences. Male suicide rates are much higher than female suicide rates in all societies, manifesting a ratio of 4:1 male to female suicides in industrialized societies. He traces these differences not to the moral structure but to the relative power of the male role over female role in society. In societies where the power of male roles over female roles is even greater than in industrialized society, like ancient China or Japan, the ratio of male to female suicides can increase from 4:1 to 10,000:1 showing it is not gender per se, but the relative power of people's position in society that is linked to their suicide rate. Higher social classes possessing more power also have higher suicide rates, reflecting the impact of social hierarchies like class as well as gender in society. Contemporary supporting evidence shows as women's power vis-a-vis men increases in the U.S. their suicide rates also increase. Similar projections would be expected comparing power differences between genders among various classes, ethnic groups or age groups to suicide rates. Specifically, Black wives are presumed to exercise more power than white wives in what has been described as a more matriarchal family structure and they should have a lower ratio than their white counterparts. One can examine differences in educational level or income of spouses to pin down the source of power. Where Durkheim would link it to their authority in the culture it may depend on their control over resources. Durkheim does not state what about social organization in industrialized or advanced societies or power is responsible for the higher suicide rate, other than their impact on the moral structure generating the social forces of integration and regulation. Thus, this suggests that he was concerned with accounting for variance in suicide rates. He never found such powerful variables within his own theory to explain the variance in the suicide rate.

Few, if any studies since Durkheim have measured either integration or regulation and examined the differences in suicide rates and calculated the variances they explained. Nor have they explored in more depth the cohesive forces uniting society and minimizing suicide or explored the nature of social bonds that unify social systems. Most subsequent scholars suggesting they were testing Durkheim's theory stretched their data, largely collected for other purposes, to unrecognizable instances of integration or regulation. So, despite the century and a quarter that has passed since Durkheim set forth his groundbreaking treatise, no work has advanced significantly or exceeded Durkheim's contribution. It is time to rigorously test and accept or leave Durkheim's theory behind for sociology to advance.

Current unification of Durkheim's theory of suicide

Durkheim had two primary objectives in *Suicide*. His first objective was to establish that suicide was socially caused, which he did successfully. His second was to develop a theory of suicide to explain the differences in suicide rates between groups in societies. The primary objectives of his theory were (a) to identify the nature of the social causes of suicide; (b) to show how these causes produce their effects, and (c) to identify the relation of social causes to individual acts of suicide (1952:li).

Durkheim identified two social forces causing suicide, integration and regulation. The status of integration as shared moral values and common practices over extended areas of individuals' lives that bind people to each other and to the group and strongly control behavior seems to adequately grasp Durkheim's intentions and reflect his notion of mechanical solidarity; however, his concept of regulation needs a different elaboration to fully take into account what processes he is trying to identify. This process refers to society's balancing appetites with opportunities so that it can successfully satisfy society's system needs by gratifying individual's socially generated appetites. Thus, this balance keeps the system of interdependencies intact, attaches individuals to that system, and reflects his notion of organic solidarity.

As the traditional interpretation and consensus model were not a good fit with the logic of Durkheim's theory, the following model is proposed. The relationship between integration and suicide rates could only be linear and inverse if highly integrated societies had no norms demanding or encouraging self-sacrifice. If the highly integrated aspect of the continuum of integration has a moderate number of norms demanding or encouraging self-sacrifice and individuals subject to those norms, a J-shaped relationship might be expected. In the third condition, where there are many such norms demanding or encouraging self-sacrifice and many people subject to those norms, a U-shaped relationship may be expected, as Durkheim found in his comparison between military and civilian populations. A failure to distinguish between highly integrated groups with varying numbers of norms requiring or encouraging self-sacrifice may result in a misleading overall conclusion. Since, highly integrated groups with no norms would have no suicides, and those with many norms affecting many people would have high suicide rates, and therefore the overall result would mask these internal differences and diminish the relationship between integration and suicide. A modern statistical test with those three sub-conditions could be employed to test the strength of those relationships. With respect to the variable regulation, the traditional U-shaped relationship is hypothesized. In addition, his theory about balancing appetites and opportunities has to include obstructions by the social structure, obstructions by the organization of society, and powerful groups that may all influence the balance between appetites and opportunities that Durkheim did not acknowledge in his theory of anomie. Since Durkheim focused exclusively on the moral control of appetites, attention now has to be given to how society is organized limiting opportunities. Therefore, in order to unify Durkheim's theory, these varying sub-conditions must be specified to fit a particular statistical model where data could properly be collected.

To be more in accord with Durkheim's intentions, there should be efforts to identify types of suicide rather than treating all suicides as the same which is the case in using official statistics. Identification of types of suicide are required in order to rigorously test Durkheim's theory. Since he used official statistics that did not differentiate different types of suicide, it is puzzling that he found relationships in the variables he examined. Further complicating the situation is that suicidal acts could be blends of the different forces, and methodology does not exist for identifying these cases.

One of the issues that need to be further developed is that Durkheim did not see that regulation was a cohesive force because it created mutual dependence. He emphasized that the specialization in the division of labor created this cohesive force during industrialization without recognizing that pre-industrial societies were also cooperative systems of mutual dependence though less specialized and that all human groups evolved as collective adaptations to their environments.

The motivation impelling individuals toward egoistic suicide comes from the process of society disintegrating and its consequences like insufficient support through tragedy resulting in byproduct feelings of purposelessness and meaninglessness. Whereas, in anomic and fatalistic suicide, it is the individual's reactions to the obstructions of society in attaining their goals that lead to the disconnection from society and subsequently suicide. For example, feelings of frustration and anger resulting from goal blockages are ways in which individuals are pushed toward suicide. The motivation impelling individuals toward altruistic suicide comes from the process of society demanding or encouraging self-sacrifice. In the case of egoistic, anomic, and fatalistic suicide, suicide is not a sanctioned behavior. Whereas, in altruistic suicide, suicide is an act conforming to society's demands of self-sacrifice or rejection. Durkheim's failure to elaborate the intervening processes and causal mechanisms between regulation and suicide makes it quite difficult to link individual acts of suicide to degrees of regulation. The limitations of testing with regard to individual suicides have already been explored and require a more thorough development of the theory before individual predictions can be made other than those already discussed. To refine the theory further, the differences in whether moral or social structures generate these forces have to be explored.

Note

1 Fatalism is omitted in this reference and is relegated to a footnote and few brief paragraphs in the text, perhaps because it is of declining importance in modern society and contributed little to the overall suicide rate. Some assert fatalistic suicide was included only for theoretical completeness or to resolve a contradiction in his theory between the earlier and later formulations completing the typology of extremes of integration and regulation and to incorporate the concept of equilibrium and balance of forces that minimizes suicides in society and aligns with his functionalist perspective. Others like Merton (1968) introduce barriers created by the social structure that limit the achievement of societal goals rather than failures of the moral structure that contribute to anomie, reflecting a more radical aspect of Durkheim.

7

CONCLUSION

Suicide extended Durkheim's analysis of the failure of modern society to develop unifying mechanisms. He viewed suicide as a consequence of weakening social bonds resulting from the erosion of the common moral system, and the diversity that specialization created in society. In addition, he viewed the lack of cohesion as a result of modern society's inability to distribute its rewards in a way that held society together and attached individuals to society. Not only did this extend Durkheim's larger system of sociology but it empirically tested some propositions from his theory of cohesion.

In *The Division of Labor*, Durkheim identified two sources of social cohesion, mechanical and organic solidarity, which held society together. In *Suicide*, he shifted the focus of cohesion from what held society together to what attached individuals to society and subsequently labeled the forces integration and regulation.

The cohesive force that held society together, which he labeled mechanical solidarity, emanated from the system of moral values or collective conscience. This force integrated the constituent elements of society into a powerful system controlling individual's behavior. The aspects of this force attaching individuals to society was identified as integration in *Suicide*, making individuals part of a larger whole society, which tightly controlled their behavior and gave meaning and purpose to their lives. When he referred to mechanical solidarity, Durkheim was specifically referring to the cohesive force that held society together; whereas, when Durkheim referred to integration, he was speaking to the social force that attaches individuals to society itself.

DOI: 10.4324/9781003669272-7

The cohesive forces described as organic solidarity emanated from the system of mutual dependence created by specialization in the division of labor and held the constituent elements of society together in a system of mutual cooperation and interdependence. Aspects of this force that attached individuals to society were described as regulation. Society motivated individuals to fulfill system needs by instilling social appetites which would be satisfied by performing their roles. By maintaining an appropriate balance between goals and means or appetites and opportunities in society, both system needs and individual appetites will be met, bonding individuals tightly to society. Regulation can be defined as the process of creating cohesion by balancing appetites with opportunities and attaching individuals to the extent that their needs are met by the system.

The forces associated with mechanical solidarity emanated from a shared moral system that controlled individual's behavior and generated a strong centripetal force integrating the constituent elements of society and attaching individuals to society was designated as "integration."

The force associated with organic solidarity emanated from the system of mutual dependence in society that held the constituent elements of society together and attached individuals to society by meeting individual's appetites. Thus, a shared moral system and system of mutual dependence form the basis of the forces integration and regulation, holding society together and attaching individuals to it.

In his study *Suicide*, he examines the consequences of diminishing cohesion in modern society on both society and individual's attachments to society. Suicide results both from the weakening social attachments and social forces impelling individuals in these conditions to end their lives. He sets forth a theory to account for these phenomena but does not examine their devastating effects on the larger society. Thus, this work extends Durkheim's larger system of sociology and proposes a systematic theory of suicide.

His two main goals were to show that suicide is socially caused and to create a theory that explains those facts. His objectives for the study were to identify the nature of the social causes of suicide, to show how these causes produce their effects, and to identify the relation of social causes to individual acts of suicide.

He was successful in demonstrating that suicide was socially caused by showing that certain structures of society produced uniform rates of suicide despite the turnover in the population. It also showed that patterns of suicide changed as the social organization of society changed and were related to people's role in that structure. These generalizations led to establishing sociology as a distinctive field of scientific study.

His theory could not address what he regarded as the central problem of sociology, which was to account for the volume of suicides with which each society was afflicted, for at least two reasons. He did not quantify the independent variables of integration and regulation and empirically measure them, and his theory accounted for only a small portion of the variance.

It did bring into focus the reality of social forces and allow us to empirically measure them, giving sociology a scientific basis. The theory was fractured, and therefore, Durkheim never developed a coherent summary specifying the various parts and how they fit together. Subsequent scholars have attempted to unify his theory but did not recognize its disjointed nature and didn't advance our understanding of his theory significantly. This book has tried to rectify and resolve the issues and somewhat unify his theory with a new understanding of the relationships between the various social forces and rates of suicide by recognizing the role both forces play in adhering individuals to society, reconceptualizing a closer tie between regulation and organic solidarity, and by drawing out the implications of the role integration played in creating suicide that required further specification of the norms of highly integrated societies that have to be taken into consideration generating hypotheses.

More modern statistics have to be cited to see if these regularities hold up in contemporary society. In addition, studies that take into account these new variables can determine if Durkheim's updated theory can increase the variance the theory can account for. These new variables include norms that demand self-sacrifice in highly integrated societies and the kind of obstacles that exist to impair satisfaction of appetites. Furthermore, indices of integration like value consensus, social conflict, and polarization can be indicative of society's disintegration as well as increases in suicide. Indices of regulation could include levels of inequality and concentrations of power and wealth, which can be related to increases in suicides as well as social disintegration, giving a new dimension to not just a new theory of suicide of individuals but a theory of the demise of societies. Refining the theory permits a more definitive test that allows us to either support or move beyond Durkheim's conceptions.

Durkheim viewed suicide as a symptom of the failure of the social forces of integration and regulation to properly attach individuals to society. The failure of regulatory forces to balance appetites with opportunities impaired democracy, capitalism, globalization, and technology's ability to deliver their benefits to society in a way that met society's collective needs and individual appetites. These benefits were not properly distributed to sufficiently hold society together and attach individuals to society, and instead, the benefits were so unevenly distributed that they could not properly contain conflict and division.

As the problems of unifying modern society increase and significant sectors of society are marginalized from political, economic, and social structures, society itself is shattering. In response, societies are moving toward totalitarianism in order to reestablish its former social cohesion by force (Fromm 1969).[1] Durkheim does not specify whether the problems emanating from regulation are the result of systems gone awry, inadequate institutions or norms, or powerful groups advancing their interests, or is an inevitable consequence of systems like capitalism. The failure of society to deliver individuals' expected standards of living or their basic physical needs is not explored by Durkheim. The dissatisfaction individuals experience also causes conflict weakening integration further tearing society apart until it totally disintegrates.

Though Durkheim struggled with these issues 125 years ago, they seem to be as relevant today if not more so than in his time. Society is still grappling with unifying mechanisms, and some concerted efforts like the United Nations have failed to establish a coherent world order. Given the existential problems of rampant inequality, global scorching, and nuclear annihilation, it is imperative to find a way to unify all life's existence on this planet. Some way to render cooperation between world societies to solve these issues has to be found.

Note

1 In addition to totalitarianism, the emergence of cults can be seen as a response to the lack of sufficient connections of people in society, and the widespread mass shootings represent a combination of social and self-annihilating events all depicting the lack of sufficient cohesive forces in modern society.

AFTERWORD

An undeveloped aspect of Durkheim's theory is exploring not only individual consequences such as suicide but how the forces of integration and regulation can also lead to society's total disintegration. The recent pandemic revealed the large-scale consequences of the loss of connections on the mental wellbeing of people in the United States. Deaths from addictions skyrocketed in those areas where people's relation to work were severed, and the rate of mass shootings increased that not only resulted in suicide but the large number of deaths of others. All of these examples reflect the disintegration of the social fabric and the hollowing out of society, creating lives of despair. Opposite to integration is increasing polarization and mistrust of others that are different, which tears society apart and creates fertile ground for civil wars. In the recent election, the people of the United States essentially voted for a suicide pact by electing a totalitarian president that will accelerate global scorching, fail to regulate AI development, and eliminate medical safeguards from pandemics through the installation of an anti-vaccine Secretary of Health and Human Services. Racism, scapegoating, political conflict, and homophobic and transphobic rhetoric all contributed to the decline in shared values that Durkheim labelled integration, a salient factor in binding society. The loss of occupations and rising inequality has hollowed out America's ability to meet the social needs of many people, reducing their bonds to society as well which Durkheim defined as regulation. Measures of both variables could be related to various societies' disintegration that would be in keeping with the spirit of Durkheim's theory. The widespread fraying of integrating and regulating forces needs to be determined to fully test Durkheim's ability to predict such circumstances.

REFERENCES

Abrutyn, Seth. 2023. "A Social Disorganizational Theory of Suicide 1." *Sociological Forum* 38(2):298–323.

Abrutyn, Seth, and Anna S. Mueller. 2016. "When Too Much Integration and Regulation Hurts: Reenvisioning Durkheim's Altruistic Suicide." *Society and Mental Health* 6(1):56–71.

Abrutyn, Seth, and Anna S. Mueller. 2018. "Toward a Cultural-Structural Theory of Suicide: Examining Excessive Regulation and Its Discontents." *Sociological Theory* 36(1):48–66.

Bearman, Peter S. 1991. "The Social Structure of Suicide." *Sociological Forum* 6(3):501–524.

Bellah, Robert N. 1959. "Durkheim and History." *American Sociological Review* 24(4)447–4613–26.

Berk, Bernard B. 2006. "Macro-Micro Relationships in Durkheim's Analysis of Egoistic Suicide." *Sociological Theory* 24(1):58–80.

Blau, Peter M. 1960. "Structural Effects." *American Sociological Review* 25(2):178–193.

Bogue, Donald J., and Elizabeth J. Bogue. 1975. *Ecological Correlation Reexamined.* Bogue.

Breault, Kevin D., and Karen Barkey. 1982. "A Comparative Analysis of Durkheim's Theory of Egoistic Suicide." *The Sociological Quarterly* 23(3):321–331.

Collins, Randall. 1988. *Theoretical Sociology.* Boston: Harcourt College Pub.

Collins, Randall. 2005. *Interaction Ritual Chains.* Princeton university press.

Danigelis, Nick, and Whitney Pope. 1979. "Durkheim's Theory of Suicide as Applied to the Family: An Empirical Test." *Social Forces* 57(4):1081–1106.

Douglas, Jack D. 1967. *The Social Meanings of Suicide.* Princeton University Press.

Duncan, Otis D., and Beverly Davis. 1953. "An Alternative to Ecological Correlation." *American Sociological Review* 18(6).

Durkheim, E. 1915. *The Elementary Forms of the Religious Life.* London: George Allen & Unwin Ltd.

Durkheim, E. 1933. *The Division of Labor in Society.* Glencoe, IL: Free Press.

Durkheim, E. 1938. *The Rules of Sociological Method.* Glencoe, IL: Free Press.

Durkheim, E. 1952. *Suicide.* London and New York: Routledge.

Emirbayer, Mustafa. 1996. "Useful Durkheim." *Sociological Theory* 14(2):109–130.

Farberow, N.L. and Shneidman, E.S. (Eds.) 1961. *The Cry for Help.* New York: Blakiston Division, McGraw-Hill.

Faris, Robert E. L, H. Warren Dunham. 1939. *Mental Disorders in Urban Areas: An Ecological Study of Schizophrenia and Other Psychoses.* University of Chicago Press.

Foucault, Michel. 1965. *Madness and Civilization: A History of Insanity in the Age of Reason.* London and New York: Routledge.

Foucault, Michel. 1975. *Discipline and Punishment: The Birth of the Prison.* Vintage Books USA.

Frankl, Viktor E. 1984. *Man's Search for Meaning: An Introduction to Logotherapy.* Touchstone.

Fromm, Erich. 1969. *Escape from Freedom.* New York: Reinhart and Winston.

Gane, Mike. 1988. *On Durkheim's Rules of Sociological Method.* London: Taylor and Francis.

Geertz, Clifford. 1973. *The Interpretation of Cultures.* Basic Books.

Gibbs, Jack P. 1968. *Suicide.* Harper & Row.

Gibbs, Jack P., and Walter T. Martin. 1958. "A Theory of Status Integration and its Relationship to Suicide." *American Sociological Review* 23(2):140–147.

Gibbs, Jack P., and Walter T. Martin. 1964. *Status Integration and Suicide.* University of Oregon Press.

Giddens, Anthony. 1972. *Emile Durkheim: Selected Writings.* Cambridge University Press Cambridge.

Hammond, John L. 1973. "Two Sources of Error in Ecological Correlations." *American Sociological Review* 38(6):764–777.

Harari, Yuval N. 2015. Sapiens: A Brief History of Humankind. Harper.

Henry, Andrew F., and James F. Short. 1954. *Suicide and Homicide: Some Economic, Sociological and Psychological Aspects of Aggression.* New York: Free Press.

Hollingshead, August B., and Frederick C. Redlich. 1958. *Social Class and Mental Illness: A Community Study.* John Wiley and Sons, Inc.

Homans, George C. 1950. *The Human Group.* Harcourt, Brace and Company.

Hynes, Eugene. 1975. "Suicide and Homo Duplex: An Interpretation of Durkheim's Typology of Suicide." *The Sociological Quarterly* 16(1):87–104.

Inkeles, Alex. 1959. "Personality and Social Structure." *Sociological Today* 2:249–276.

Johnson, Barclay D. 1965. "Durkheim's One Cause of Suicide." *American Sociological Review* 30(6):875–886.

Jones, Susan S. 2013. *Durkheim Reconsidered.* John Wiley & Sons.

Landecker, Werner S. 1950. "Types of Integration and their Measurement." *American Journal of Sociology* 56(4):332–340.

Lester, David. 1989. "A Test of Durkheim's Theory of Suicide using Data from Modern Nations." *International Journal of Comparative Sociology* 30(3-4):235–238.

Lester, David. 1992. "A Test of Durkheim's Theory of Suicide in Primitive Societies." *Suicide and Life-Threatening Behavior* 22(3):388–395.

Lester, David. 1994. *Emile Durkheim Le Suicide 100 Years Later*. Philadelphia: The Charles Press.

Linton, Ralph. 1936. *The Study of Man*. New York: Appleton-Century.

Malczewski, Eric. 2013. "Durkheim's Sui Generis Reality and the Central Subject Matter of Social Science." pp. 161–175 in *Social Theories of History and Histories of Social Theory*. United Kingdom: Emerald Group Publishing Limited.

May, Rollo. 1977. *The Meaning of Anxiety*. New York: WW Norton & Co.

Merton, Robert K. 1968. "Social Structure and Anomie" in *Social Theory and Social Structure*. New York: Free Press.

Meštrović, Stjepan. 1994. *Emile Durkheim and the Reformation of Sociology*. Rowman & Littlefield Publishers.

Muntaner, C., et al. 1996. "Social Class and Suicidal Behavior: The Relevance of Socioeconomic Status to Durkheim's Theory of Suicide," *Social Science & Medicine*.

Newcomb, Theodore M. 1953. "An Approach to the Study of Communicative Acts." *Psychological Review* 60(6):393.

Nolan, Patrick, and Gerhard E. Lenski. 2004. *Human Societies: An Introduction to Macrosociology*. London and New York: Routledge.

Parsons, Talcott. 1949. *The Structure of Social Action*. Glencoe, IL: Free Press.

Pearce, Frank, and Thomas M. Kemple. 2001. *The Radical Durkheim, 2nd Edition*. Canadian Scholars Press

Pescosolido, Bernice A., and Sharon Georgianna. 1989. "Durkheim, Suicide, and Religion: Toward a Network Theory of Suicide." *American Sociological Review* 54(1):33–48. doi: 10.2307/2095660.

Pescosolido, Bernice A., and Robert Mendelsohn. 1986. "Social Causation or Social Construction of Suicide? An Investigation into the Social Organization of Official Rates." *American Sociological Review* 51(1):80–100. doi: 10.2307/2095479.

Pickering, W., and Geoffrey Walford. 2000. *Durkheim's Suicide: A Century of Research and Debate*. London and New York: Routledge.

Pope, Whitney. 1976. *Durkheim's Suicide: A Classic Analyzed*. University of Chicago Press.

Porpora, Douglas V. 2015. *Reconstructing Sociology: The Critical Realist Approach*. Cambridge University Press.

Riesman, David, Nathan Glazer and Reuel Denney. 2020. *The Lonely Crowd*. Yale University Press.

Robinson, William S. 1950. "Ecological Correlations and the Behavior of Individuals." American Sociological Review 15(3):351–357.

Scheff, Thomas J. 1990. *Microsociology: Discourse, Emotion, and Social Structure*. University of Chicago Press.

Scheff, Thomas J. 1997. *Emotions, the Social Bond, and Human Reality*. Cambridge University Press.

Scheff, Thomas J. 2011. "The Catastrophe of Scientism in Social/Behavioral Science." *Contemporary Sociology* 40(3):264–268.

Scheff, Thomas J., and Susanne Retzinger. 1991. *Emotions and Violence: Shame and Rage in Destructive Conflicts*. Lexington Books.

Seeman, Melvin. 1991. "Alienation and Anomie." *Measures of Personality and Social Psychological Attitudes* 1:291–371.

Selvin, Hanan C. 1965. *Durkheim's "Suicide": Further Thoughts on a Methodological Classic*. Prentice Hall.

Shils, Edward A., and Morris Janowitz. 1948. "Cohesion and Disintegration in the Wehrmacht in World War II." *Public Opinion Quarterly* 12(2):280–315.

Simpson, Miles E., and George H. Conklin. 1989. "Socioeconomic Development, Suicide and Religion: A Test of Durkheim's Theory of Religion and Suicide." *Social Forces* 67(4):945–964.

Stack, Steven. 1978. "Suicide: A Comparative Analysis." *Social Forces* 57(2):644–653.

Stack, Steven. 1980. "Religion and Suicide: A Reanalysis." *Social Psychiatry* 15:65–70.

Stack, Steven. 1983. "A Comparative Analysis of Durkheim's Theory of Egoistic Suicide: A Comment." *The Sociological Quarterly* 24(4):625–627.

Stack, Steven. 2000. "Suicide: A 15-Year Review of the Sociological Literature. Part I: Cultural and Economic Factors." *Suicide and Life-Threatening Behavior* 30(2):145–162.

Stack, Steven, and Augustine J. Kposowa. 2008. "The Association of Suicide Rates with Individual-Level Suicide Attitudes: A Cross-National Analysis." *Social Science Quarterly* 89(1):39–59.

Stouffer, Samuel A., Edward A. Suchman, Leland C. DeVinney, Shirley A. Star, and Robin M. Williams Jr. 1949. *The American Soldier: Adjustment during Army Life*. Princeton University Press.

Swanson, Guy E. 1969. *The Birth of the Gods the Origin of Primitive Beliefs*. University of Michigan Press.

Takla, Tendzin N., and Whitney Pape. 1985. "The Force Imagery in Durkheim: The Integration of Theory, Metatheory, and Method." *Sociological Theory* 3(1):74–88.

Toffler, Alvin. 1984. *Future Shock*. Bantam Books.

Travis, Robert. 1990. "Halbwachs and Durkheim: A Test of Two Theories of Suicide." *British Journal of Sociology* 41(2):225–243.

Turner, Jonathan H. 1990. "Emile Durkheim's Theory of Social Organization." *Social Forces* 68(4):1089–1103.

Turner, Stephen. 1986. *The Search for a Methodology of Social Science*. Springer.

Van Poppel, Frans, and Lincoln H. Day. 1996. "A Test of Durkheim's Theory of Suicide--without Committing the "Ecological Fallacy"." *American Sociological Review* 61(3):500–507.

White, Leslie A. 1949. *The Science of Culture: A Study of Man and Civilization*. Grove Press, Inc.

White, Leslie A. 1959. The Evolution of Culture: The Development of Civilization to the Fall of Rome. McGraw-Hill.

Wray, Matt, Cynthia Colen and Bernice Pescosolido. 2011. "The Sociology of Suicide." *Annual Review of Sociology* 37(1):505–528.

INDEX